Coming Out

German Film Classics

Series Editors
Gerd Gemünden, Dartmouth College
Johannes von Moltke, University of Michigan

Advising Editors
Anton Kaes, University of California-Berkeley
Eric Rentschler, Harvard University

Editorial Board
Hester Baer, University of Maryland
Mattias Frey, University of Kent
Rembert Hüser, Goethe University, Frankfurt
Claudia Lenssen, Journalist and Film Critic, Berlin
Cristina Nord, Berlinale Forum
Brad Prager, University of Missouri
Reinhild Steingröver, Eastman School of Music

Also in the series:

COMING OUT

KYLE FRACKMAN

CAMDEN HOUSE

The open access version of this book is made possible by the UBC
Open Access Fund for Humanities and Social Sciences Research
CC-BY-NC

First published 2022 by Camden House

Camden House is an imprint of Boydell & Brewer Inc.
668 Mt. Hope Avenue, Rochester, NY 14620, USA
and of Boydell & Brewer Limited
PO Box 9, Woodbridge, Suffolk IP12 3DF, UK
www.boydellandbrewer.com

Cover image: Philipp's agitated contemplation of his reflection
shows his continued wrestling with his sexual identity. Used by
permission © DEFA-Stiftung/Martin Schlesinger.

ISBN-13: 978-1-64014-089-9

Library of Congress Cataloging-in-Publication Data

CIP data is available from the Library of Congress.

This publication is printed on acid-free paper.
Printed in the United States of America.

Publication of this book was supported by a grant from the
German Film Institute (GFI) of the University of Michigan
Department of Germanic Languages & Literatures.

CONTENTS

ACKNOWLEDGMENTS

Matthias Freihof and Dirk Kummer generously met with me multiple times to talk about their experiences in the GDR and with *Coming Out*. I thank the following individuals for their parts in helping me find information or moving the project along: at the DEFA-Stiftung Barbara Barlet and Gudrun Scherp; at the DEFA Film Library Hiltrud Schulz and Skyler Arndt-Briggs. Thanks to support from the University of British Columbia (UBC) Faculty of Arts, I have worked with several invaluable research assistants: Jonathan Allen, Steve Commichau, Morris Ho, Olga Holin, and Anna Westpfahl. Helena Kudzia helped with a Polish translation. I appreciate the exchanges about this film I have had with many colleagues, including Katherine Bowers, Stephen Guy-Bray, Sebastian Heiduschke, Ilinca Iuraşcu, Gregory Mackie, Ervin Malakaj, Vin Nardizzi, Alessandra Santos, and Evan Torner. Finally, I am grateful for the support from Chris Beaubien, who has watched *Coming Out* with me numerous times and is always generously eager to hear about my discoveries.

Parts of this book appeared in different form in "The East German Film *Coming Out* (1989) as Melancholic Reflection and Hopeful Projection," *German Life and Letters* 71, no. 4 (2018): 452–72, and "Persistent Ambivalence: Theorizing Queer East German Studies," *Journal of Homosexuality* 66, no. 5 (2019): 669–89.

The book's cover image appears by permission © DEFA-Stiftung/Martin Schlesinger.

This book draws on research supported by the Social Sciences and Humanities Research Council of Canada (SSHRC). The open access version of this book is made possible by the UBC Open Access Fund for Humanities and Social Sciences Research.

Coming Out

The fall of the Berlin Wall on November 9, 1989, is an event known to most people familiar with Western European—even world—history of the late twentieth century. Seemingly near miraculous at the time, as even a year or two earlier almost no one would have predicted it, it hastened the end of the Cold War and led to the unification of Germany. These earthshaking changes were mirrored in a much more subtle, even hidden set of developments in the society and culture of the German Democratic Republic (GDR, East Germany) in the months and years leading up to that point. One of these was an increasing public tolerance of homosexuality. So it is ironic that the premiere of the first and only gay-themed feature film to be made in the GDR, and the first film to show an extended same-sex sexual encounter, occurred on the very night of the fall of the Wall, that same November 9, and was overshadowed by it. Although that film, *Coming Out*, directed by Heiner Carow with a screenplay by Wolfram Witt, was critically acclaimed and won—among other awards—the Silver Bear and Teddy at the 1990 Berlin International Film Festival or Berlinale, the attention it received was undoubtedly attenuated by the world-changing political events taking place around its premiere.

Coming Out is a monumental film. This film—both its story and the filmic way it is told—is at once typical and extremely unusual for the cinema of the GDR and for the director who created it. *Coming Out* is an emotional engagement with the state of the GDR in the late 1980s, using melodrama and manipulation of genre to depict the plight of LGBTQ+ people.[1] It is a queer story told using queer techniques; it uses a conventional, cisheteronormative form to deliver queer content, turning what could have been a traditional heterosexual love story into an unconventional queer story. As I discuss below, the film plays with genre expectations, mise-en-scène, cinematography, and sound and music to change the viewer's expectations and to make the narrative of the film itself an example of queerness in a field of supposed normality. *Coming Out* resists narrative closure, opting instead for a hopeful, yet critical, portrayal of the characters' world. In what follows, I will demonstrate how Carow's film achieves this, while also providing additional background on details in the film and its context in 1989 East Germany.

A brief synopsis of *Coming Out* reinforces the melodramatic nature of the story. The film proceeds chronologically and opens with the aftermath of a New Year's Eve suicide attempt by Matthias (Dirk Kummer), who decided to end his life because of his homosexuality. The focal character, Philipp Klahrmann (Matthias Freihof), is a young teacher who enters a relationship with one of his colleagues, Tanja (Dagmar Manzel), who eventually gets pregnant by him. The unexpected appearance of Tanja's friend Jakob (Axel Wandtke), with whom he had been romantically involved, sends Philipp into an emotional tailspin. He begins to explore gay bars, which facilitates the start of his relationship with Matthias. The parallel, competing identities that Philipp tries to maintain are unsustainable, and his personal and professional lives fall into disarray. He is rejected by Matthias, Tanja, and his mother (Walfriede Schmitt). Along the way, Philipp learns more about queer life in East Berlin and meets characters like the waiter Achim (Michael Gwisdek), waitress Charlotte (famed trans icon Charlotte von Mahlsdorf), and Walter (Werner Dissel), a victim of antiqueer persecution under the Nazis and dedicated to the socialist cause, all of whom contribute both to a rehabilitation of Philipp's character and an improvement of the circumstances in which he is struggling. By the end of the film, his relationships with Tanja and Matthias have ended, but he is content and certain in his identity, although homophobia and its consequences have disrupted the lives of Philipp, Matthias, Tanja, and many others in the film. At the same time, the image of the GDR the film conveys is one of a society in which sexual and racial minorities must struggle. East German public tolerance of LGBTQ+ people slowly increased in the 1980s, but the film also demonstrates that problems like sexism and far-right, racist violence had not been eliminated.

Heiner Carow and Film's Revolutionary Potential

Heiner Carow (1929–97) was a fitting director for this project. Before *Coming Out*, he had created several films for DEFA (Deutsche Film Aktiengesellschaft, German Film Corporation) that, for one reason or another, had made waves. He worked in multiple genres and styles, ranging from neorealism to melodrama, but it was to melodrama that he repeatedly returned. Carow's first feature film, *Sheriff Teddy* (1957), and his second, *They Called Him Amigo* (*Sie nannten ihn Amigo*, 1958), focus on the experiences of young people, with clear evocations of Gerhard Lamprecht's *Somewhere in Berlin* (*Irgendwo in Berlin*, 1946) with its groups of unsupervised children roving around a partially destroyed city. Unlike the rubble films in the Western occupation zones, Ute Wölfel has argued, the youth-focused rubble films from the Soviet occupation zone convey messages about the importance of society and the young people's role in the collective.[2] One can draw a line from these earlier works to *Coming Out*, in that the films tell stories about the importance of social integration and communal support. Carow's film *The Russians Are Coming* (*Die Russen kommen*, 1968) was banned by censors after the Eleventh Plenum of the Central Committee of East Germany's ruling Socialist Unity Party (Sozialistische Einheitspartei Deutschlands, SED), which met in 1965–66 to set new cultural policy, and only finally released in 1987. That film, which focuses on a teenaged character who joins the Wehrmacht and faces a deep psychological crisis, was destroyed, supposedly because it highlights a regular Nazi follower and because of its modernist influence. (Evelyn Carow, a well-known DEFA editor [including on *Coming Out*]) and Carow's spouse, saved a copy of the film.[3])

The last two decades of the GDR saw both Carow's greatest success and a heightened willingness on his part to publicly debate the conditions of cultural production in the GDR and to raise questions in his films about the society's shortcomings. In 1973, DEFA released Carow's film *The Legend of Paul and Paula* (*Die Legende von Paul und Paula*, 1972), which quickly became the GDR's biggest hit. Now a cult favorite, the film is a tragic romance between the title characters, set to the rock music of the band The Puhdys. Andrea Rinke interprets it as a "radical plea for individual self-determination, diametrically opposed to the message of socialist realism."[4] Carow was one of a number of filmmakers who advocated for more freedom in how they could approach their material, participating in an ongoing public debate—in venues like the journal *Film und Fernsehen*—about the usefulness of socialist realism and which styles best facilitated a connection to the audience.[5] "Lenin speaks of film art as the most important, and he meant the art's revolutionary potential," Carow argued. "It is precisely this revolutionary role that contemporary film art is not playing."[6] Carow maintained that film art could do more for society. In *Until Death Do Us Part* (*Bis daß der Tod euch scheidet*, 1978, released 1979), Carow turned again to melodrama to tell the story of a troubled urban marriage and the challenges that still beset people (especially women) within socialism. Like Carow's other films of the 1980s, *So Many Dreams* (*So viele Träume*, 1986) is a story about the complicated choices many faced within socialist society.

Although Carow had risen to be part of the artistic establishment, becoming vice president of the Academy of Arts (1982–91), he received pushback on some of his directorial choices. One of Carow's unrealized film projects was *Paule Panke*, a film adaptation of the band Pankow's rock musical of the early 1980s. In an interview, Carow maintained that the difficulties and rejection of the project were due to the script's inclusion of a gay character. Carow's experience with *Paule Panke* influenced his decision to make *Coming Out*, leading him to think defiantly that if the mere appearance of a gay character was a problem, then he was going to focus on the issue head on.[7] Carow, however, still had to satisfy multiple layers of the DEFA bureaucracy before his idea for *Coming Out* could come to fruition.

By the time he worked on *Coming Out*, Carow had become part of the major debates about filmmaking in the GDR. He had created noteworthy, impactful films, frequently using the techniques of melodrama to tell compelling stories about characters, especially young people, in difficult situations. Erika Richter (1938–2020), a DEFA dramaturge who worked with Carow on the *Paule Panke* material and on *Coming Out*, wrote after Carow's death in 1997 that he "was a born dramatist, but the dramatist lives off of conflicts, and that is something GDR society was hard-pressed to accept."[8] Thus, in many ways, Carow was well positioned for this film: someone with a degree of clout and artistic freedom who was likely from its start to challenge rules and make many people uncomfortable.

Homosexuality in East Germany

Homosexual acts between men were criminalized in East Germany until 1968, when the relevant law (§175) was removed from the criminal code. Nonetheless, the GDR regime continued to view LGBTQ+ people as a threat to society. Many lesbians and gay men were harassed and placed under surveillance by the Ministry for State Security, or Stasi. When Rosa von Praunheim's campy 1971 film *Nicht der Homosexuelle ist pervers, sondern die Situation, in der er lebt* (*It Is Not the Homosexual Who Is Perverse but the Society in Which He Lives*) was broadcast on West German television in 1972 and 1973, it sparked a gay rights movement—including the founding of the first queer rights group in East Germany, the Homosexual

Interest Community of Berlin (HIB)—that continued in various forms through the 1970s and 1980s despite state efforts to quash it. Much of this activism had to remain private and could take place only in private homes or under the guise of birthday parties in rented rooms, since this form of collective organizing was illegal.

Although *Coming Out* was the GDR's first feature film to focus on homosexuality, Carow's film came a year after a short documentary, *The Other Love* (*Die andere Liebe*), was produced by the German Hygiene Museum in Dresden in collaboration with the DEFA Studio for Documentary Film. That film, directed by Helmut Kißling and Axel Otten, was East Germany's first sustained filmic engagement with homosexuality. The arrival of *The Other Love* in 1988 marked a—by Western standards—belated cinematic sexual revolution for queer representation. Not only had West German (and Western, more broadly) media long depicted LGBTQ+ people in public—from heterosexist or more neutral analyses in the weekly *Der Spiegel* to the edgy 1981 film *Taxi zum Klo* (*Taxi to the Toilet*, directed by Frank Ripploh), which also follows a gay teacher—but there had been growing public activism by LGBTQ+ people in the GDR since the mid-1970s. Most attention to queerness highlighted men's experiences; and unlike *The Other Love*, *Coming Out* too did not explicitly focus on lesbians or female same-sex affection.[9]

Carow and *Coming Out*'s scriptwriter, Wolfram Witt, were committed to creating a film that reached beyond members of the LGBTQ+ community in the GDR. As Witt told an interviewer for the newspaper *Junge Welt*, "We especially want to reach people who, in whatever way, encounter the problem of 'being different.' And that is nothing unique, because that affects us all."[10] Carow and Witt—who also worked with Carow on *So Many Dreams* (1986) and *Verfehlung* (*The Mistake*, 1991)—are skilled at subtextual elements that recur or can be read in multiple ways. This approach was common in East Germany, where film and other cultural works could face institutional barriers and censorship.

All films made by the DEFA Studios navigated multiple layers of approvals before they could be produced and released. *Coming Out* underwent heightened scrutiny since it dealt with a controversial topic. Even under normal circumstances, films could encounter long unexplained production delays or outright cancellation. After the Eleventh Plenum, filmmakers faced more censorship, which led many to avoid taking risks that might put their projects and careers in danger.[11] In 1971, Erich Honecker replaced Walter Ulbricht as leader of the GDR. That same year, Honecker made a speech declaring that there were "no taboos" in artistic production, with the considerable caveat that the art must come from a socialist perspective.[12] Filmmakers could now, in theory, address everyday socialism, its challenges, and the individuals living in the socialist system. Many of the freedoms supposedly gained at this moment were short lived, however. Fifteen or sixteen years after Honecker's speech, when Carow began actively working toward the film's production, the director knew it would be a challenge to make *Coming Out*. To persuade the decision makers, he secured three strong expert opinions in support of the film's first round of approvals.

The three opinions—from sociologist Kurt Starke, neurologist and psychiatrist Maria Planitzer, and legal scholar Karl-Heinz Schöneburg—convey endorsements of the project but concentrate on different aspects. Starke argued that the film could provide positive social support for gay East Germans, noting that views of homosexuality had changed significantly in recent years, especially among young people.[13] Acknowledging that there was increased awareness of issues related to homosexuality, Starke maintained that *Coming Out* could and should contribute to the dismantling of prejudices against homosexuals but that it should not engage with the topic of HIV/AIDS, since the coupling of these themes had had negative consequences and tended to reinforce prejudices.[14] Although HIV/AIDS does not come up in *Coming Out*, contemplating the topic in relation to the film is not wholly unreasonable. It was a topic of which some in the public must have been aware, especially since most East Germans had access to West German broadcasting, which provided broader coverage of the HIV/AIDS epidemic than was available in the East. There had been some discussion of HIV/AIDS in East German media, including in newspapers and on television shows, but it was only in 1987 that there was the first public discussion of HIV/AIDS as something relevant to East Germans (and not just the imperialist West). The other two expert opinions focused on different parts of *Coming Out*'s potential. Stating clearly that homosexuality is not a disease or disorder, Planitzer represented the medical profession, which comprised practitioners who were responsible for contributing to homosexuals' persecution, including under the Nazis.[15] Schöneburg concerned himself with the legal position of homosexuals in the GDR and the related effects on society (including their higher suicide rate).[16] Both Planitzer and Schöneburg touched upon the antifascist potential of the film and its relationship to one of the GDR's core tenets, including the crucial scene in which Walter tells Philipp about his experience under the Nazis.[17]

These expert opinions reveal something about the world of the GDR into which the film would be released. Although the three testimonials took distinct approaches, Planitzer, Schöneburg, and Starke agreed that a film like *Coming Out* was needed in the GDR, for multiple reasons. These included ongoing social discrimination, historical injustices, and the state's responsibility to address the concerns of all members of socialist society. It was the experts' insistence on the interconnectedness of citizens in socialism—and on the connection between the discrimination and violence that LGBTQ+ people were facing in the GDR and the Nazis' horrific treatment of their predecessors—that was most influential. Hans Dieter Mäde, director of the DEFA Studios from 1976 to 1989, had told Carow that he would never allow such a film to be produced. But Carow sent the materials about the project, including the expert opinions in support of the screenplay, directly to Kurt Hager, the chief ideologist of the SED and a member of the Politburo, whose favorable reception of the subject's links to Communist Party history was decisive.

The Distress of Coming Out

The opening scenes of *Coming Out* demonstrate how dire the situation could be for LGBTQ+ people, although the film begins with a jubilant moment. New Year's Eve fireworks illuminate the sky, and revelers walk in the temporarily brightly lit night. Amid the apparent celebration, an ambulance quickly proceeds through the Berlin streets. Its siren wailing, the ambulance determinedly crosses the screen from different vantage points, continuing past the ongoing pyrotechnics and the pedestrians, evoking the existence of individual suffering even at a time of urban celebration (fig. 1). We cut to a hospital as a young man, brought by the ambulance, is wheeled down a hallway toward a treatment room. The young man, Matthias Seifert, has attempted suicide, and his stomach must be pumped. A physician (played by one of the experts who supported the film's approval by the censors, Maria Planitzer) and nurses work to help him while trying to get him to cooperate (fig. 2). Their voices direct Matthias to "Swallow!" and "Don't forget to breathe!" The discomfort of the scene escalates as the medical professionals maneuver a tube down Matthias's throat to pump his stomach. Tears run down his face as the pump does its work. The viewer gets some relief when the film cuts to the following scene, in which Matthias lies on a hospital gurney in a drab hallway (fig. 3). Fluorescent lights flicker above Matthias, who is utterly alone. The physician from the previous scene approaches Matthias and asks him multiple times what drove him to attempt suicide. Crying, Matthias reveals the reason: "I'm gay. I'm a homosexual." "Oh, Matthias," the physician says. "Don't cry because of that," as she strokes his face and tries to

Figure 1. An ambulance hurries a patient to the hospital while East Berlin celebrates the New Year.

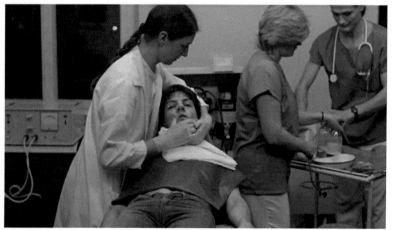

Figure 2. The physician prepares to pump Matthias's stomach after his suicide attempt.

comfort him. The film then cuts to a shot of a busy intersection, the sky a pervasive gray, and the film's title: COMING OUT (fig. 4).

This sequence makes for a jarring beginning; the scenes display repeated juxtapositions. A stationary camera captures the ambulance

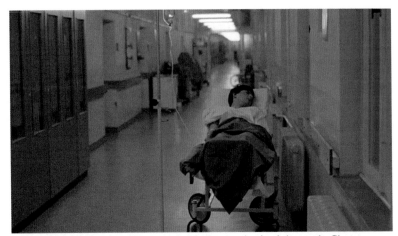

Figure 3. Prevented from committing suicide, Matthias is isolated and alone in the Charité hospital.

Figure 4. This frame emphasizes the title's unusual use of an English phrase against the background of an ordinary, gray Berlin day.

passing through Prenzlauer Berg. It turns a corner and passes groups of people enjoying the celebration. Whatever unknown distress may be taking place within the ambulance is unaffected by the new year. The ambulance seems small, as it persistently makes its way to its destination. As it weaves its way through the merrymaking, it sets up a miniature version of the melodrama we will see enacted in *Coming Out*: the experience of LGBTQ+ East Germans within the larger society. The lives of people (like Matthias), along with their crises, go on largely unacknowledged by the rest of society. Normality, in this case the festivity of the holiday, continues despite the distress of the minority. The opening sequence prompts questions about queerness and its relations to society and whether queerness can fit into that society. What does someone like Matthias need from his society? The suicide attempt is a prompt for the question; the rest of the film is an effort to move toward an answer.

A startling opening to a film was not unusual for Carow. His cult hit *The Legend of Paul and Paula* opens with the abrupt demolition of multiple buildings. It is also in keeping with Carow's other films to begin with external shots, providing an establishment of location and tone (even ironically), as is the case in *The Russians Are Coming, Until Death Do Us Part*, and *The Mistake*. The opening sequence of *Coming Out* illustrates the material demands of the film, too. Its shooting took place during one of the most unforgiving parts of the year in Berlin: the autumn and early winter were cold, wet, and—important for the cameras—dark. Carow and production leader Horst Hartwig did their best to shoot the film on imported (also more expensive and difficult to acquire) Kodak film, since the readily available East German ORWO stock had limited sensitivity and required significantly more lighting.[18] More than following Carow's custom, though, the opening sequence of *Coming Out* delivers a spectacle that introduces the subject of the film while also setting up dynamics of the story. These qualities include the film's depiction of citizens' complex positions within socialism—one of Carow's touchstones— and the film's underlying use of melodrama. The camerawork, editing, music, and mise-en-scène boldly capture the viewer's attention and vividly render the subject.

What plays out in these first minutes is the drama of one individual's fate within a system that does not want him. One of the primary ways the GDR defined an individual's use to society was their capacity to participate in procreative heterosexuality and thus in the workforce and the economy. In this way, the GDR acted on its "reason of state," to use Michel Foucault's term in describing biopolitics—that is, ways to control citizens' lives—or, as Jasbir Puar puts it, to "enable some forms of living and inhibit others."[19] When Matthias responds to the physician's question about why he tried to kill himself, he replies matter-of-factly, although through sobs: "I'm gay. I'm a homosexual." His reasoning is clear to him and becomes clear to the physician and the viewer. Stephen Best has observed that gayness can function as a social exterminator, effecting death—social or perhaps otherwise—once the truth is known and to some degree even before it is acknowledged.[20] Matthias's gayness, which is the impetus for the attempt on his own life, constitutes a failure to thrive in his world. His suicide attempt is not an example of the popular assertion that the GDR regime drove countless citizens to their self-inflicted deaths. The GDR did regularly have an unusually high suicide rate, about 50 percent higher than that of the Federal Republic to the west, also ranking high in comparison with some other Eastern Bloc nations.[21] Recent scholarship maintains that political factors did not play the decisive role that has long been assumed.[22] Nonetheless, the aftermath of the suicide attempt is the prologue to the protagonist Philipp's story.

Meant to be sympathetic, the doctor's response to Matthias's near loss of life can be read as inadequate if not dismissive. Standing in for the (state) care that the woman playing the doctor (Maria Planitzer) also represented in her expert testimonial for the film's approval, the physician commiserates with Matthias and strokes his face. Yet, her reply to Matthias's justification for suicide is banal. Regardless, the physician's action is unique in GDR media; it approaches what Chris Ingraham calls a "gesture of concern," wherein the "value lies less in being effective than in being expressive."²³ In his reading of *Coming Out*, Denis M. Sweet argues that the motif of suicide—which is dropped and never again brought up in the film—is a way both to remind the viewer of "homosexuals' inherent suffering" and to do the work of activating the viewer's compassion, even if homosexuality is something the viewer may find disgusting or pathetic.²⁴ The compassionate physician enacts tolerance.

The film's title, the simple English phrase "coming out," sets and subverts expectations for what the film will do. The film's title frame (fig. 4) becomes a description and a warning for both queer and nonqueer viewers of the film, underlining the reality of the present. *Coming Out* begins with the effects of a character's suicide attempt, standing in for the metaphorical and social suicide that queer people could cause if they come out. The film's title is a caption for what has just occurred, as well as a preview for Philipp's story to come: in other words, "this is what coming out looks like." The shots over which the title is displayed and those that follow, including when the viewer initially sees Philipp, deliver emotional relief from the opening sequence, although the relevance of Matthias's experience in the opening sequence will remain unknown to the viewer for some time. Although it was not common, use of the phrase "coming out" increased in German in the late 1980s and early 1990s. The phrase had been used sparingly in East German media, but it was more widespread in West German media of the 1980s, owing to influence from English-language sources. David Brandon Dennis interprets the fact that Carow gave his film an English-language title to be an example of how "Western discourses on lesbian and gay liberation form at least part of its cultural intertext."²⁵

Although the film's title is evidence of its engagement with international developments in talking about queerness, by showing one version of what coming out looks and feels like, the liberatory and, in a limited way, documentary work that the film carries out came late when compared to Western media. Within the decade following the 1969 Stonewall rebellion in New York, LGBTQ+ people saw positive representation in Rosa von Praunheim's *It Is Not the Homosexual*, mentioned above, and in US films like *Word Is Out* (1977) and *Gay USA* (1978), which thematized the idea of the "closet" and the act of "coming out" of it. *It Is Not the Homosexual* had stirred audiences, especially gay men, with its concluding exhortation—referring to the practice of sex in public restrooms—to come "Out of the toilets! Into the streets!" ("Raus aus den Toiletten! Rein in die Strassen!"). There were many films made in the 1980s that sought to normalize and sterilize the same LGBTQ+ people who had been portrayed as killers or other deviants in films like Alfred Hitchcock's *Rope* (1948) and William Wyler's *The Children's Hour* (1961). Queer people were the source of comedy in films like *La Cage aux Folles* (1978, directed by Édouard Molinaro) and *Porky's* (1981, directed by Bob Clark) as well as sexless or hypersexual figures in pictures like *Beverly Hills Cop* (1984, directed by Martin Brest). The 1980s and early 1990s also saw films like *Cruising* (1980, directed by William Friedkin), a fundamentally antiqueer film in its linking of gayness and violence, and many others, like *Parting Glances* (1986, directed by Bill Sherwood), that expressed the collective mourning for a generation ravaged by, first, social stigma, and then by HIV/AIDS.

The logic of the closet implies, if it does not require, the goal of coming out. "'Closetedness' itself," Eve Kosofsky Sedgwick writes, "is a performance initiated as such by the speech act of a silence—not a particular silence, but a silence that accrues particularity by fits and starts, in relation to the discourse that surrounds and differentially constitutes it."[26] Where and when one is closeted or out or able to come out will depend on individual circumstances and social expectations. With the teleological assumption of the title, one could expect the same (coming out) of the film's narrative. What *Coming Out* performs, however, is a reminder of the complicatedness and continuality of coming out. Coming out can be and usually is eternally incomplete, as long as the assumption of the dominant sexuality reigns.

Melodrama and Its Excesses

Viewers would be right to find the opening scenes melodramatic. *Coming Out* is a queer story communicated via a variation on a conventional heteronormative form. At its core, *Coming Out* is a queerly melodramatic work: not a pure melodrama, but rather a pastiche of different devices, genres, and styles. The agitated beginning, with its alternating emotional highs and lows, from the New Year's Eve celebration to the plaintive sexual admission, the severely depressive act of attempted suicide, Matthias's outpouring of despair over his homosexuality—all point to a melodramatic structure. Although it has a longer history in theater, the term *melodrama* began in the 1920s to be applied to films that focus on domestic and family-related storylines and their attendant aesthetic qualities. Melodramas often foreground aspects of gender—for instance, having central women characters—and their plots tend to be advanced by stereotypical or exaggerated characters and circumstances.[27] These films use less-developed characters who are not necessarily "autonomous individuals" but rather who frequently serve as links in the narrative chain, as film scholar Thomas Elsaesser writes.[28] One finds protagonists who are often unable to change the course of events determined by social circumstances.

DEFA, too, had a tradition of melodramas. Early DEFA films of the 1940s and 1950s built upon the filmic vocabulary and idiom of Nazi-era melodramas (even if many of them had antifascist objectives), which in turn had developed those of the Weimar era. Melodrama was a cinematic tool that could rehabilitate masculine images in the wake of Nazism's discrediting of German masculinity and serve the purposes of antifascist education.[29] Like Elsaesser, Barton Byg notes that these narratives are often built around a cisheterosexual love story and the concerns of a female protagonist, especially the distress caused by the man she loves.[30] Although *Coming Out* is far removed from the melodramas of the 1940s and 1950s and earlier, it shares traits with many past melodramas. Some of these overlaps in the film become opportunities for queering the expectations prompted by genre devices.

One typical feature of classic melodramas that *Coming Out* shares but renders queerly is the cisheterosexual love triangle or love story. Conventionally, this involved a woman who had to choose between two complementary men, or between a man and some moral choice, such as whether to participate in a villain's criminal plan.[31] *Coming Out* involves a love triangle, but not a typical one between two heterosexual men competing for a woman, a structure it subverts. The classic structure would expect Tanja, Philipp's erstwhile girlfriend, at the center of the interactions. Instead, *Coming Out* puts Philipp at the center, which allows for a foregrounding of his emotional and practical concerns regarding his emerging sexual identity. The other points of the triangle are Tanja and Matthias, representing, respectively, the two possibilities for Philipp's future: his conventional (heterosexual) life versus his newfound homosexual life. Tanja's position in her relationship with Philipp and its outcomes (like her pregnancy) are subordinated to Philipp's self-exploration. Hester Baer contends that the film's use of the structure of the relationship film "orient[s] spectators within a familiar plot scheme and secure[s] sympathy for the film's protagonists in order to then demonstrate the harm perpetuated by precisely these normative conventions."[32] *Coming Out* expands upon its queering of the love or relationship story by using devices of romantic or screwball comedies, as I illustrate below.

Melodrama is at its heart a queer form. Jonathan Goldberg argues compellingly that melodramatic aesthetics are especially apt for communicating impossible circumstances and choices, writing that it frequently permits sexuality to take center stage.[33] Goldberg's explication relies on melodrama's embedded musicality as well as narrative and structural devices whose "effect is to open a space of irresolution."[34] Melodramas traditionally marry music and drama, offering the former as a parallel track to the latter. Crucially, too, melodramas contain multiplicities—love relationships, subplots, motivations—that point to its excessiveness, one of its queer attributes.[35] Keeping in mind Goldberg's observation that "[the music] intimates that alongside the everyday world there is another"[36] and paying special attention to the use of music in *Coming Out* can give us clues about what else may be taking place. *Coming Out*'s story is accompanied by a series of musical choices that on their face are sufficient for the needs of the soundtrack but also often have deeper significance. Here, music allows for subtle critiques or allegories that could not be elevated to the surface for fear of censorship. Instead of producing clarity, Goldberg argues, melodramatic tropes "sustain irresolution."[37] Melodramatic form is not "one that offers happy endings that confirm the ability of the social as presently constituted to make good on goodness."[38] In *Coming Out*, as Katrin Sieg has argued, Philipp discovers that his homosexuality is an incarnation of the irreconcilability of "the individual right to happiness and social reproduction."[39] *Coming Out* does depend on the viewer's expectation of certain outcomes. This melodramatic queer story, however, subverts the kind of certainty or moral clarity that critics like Peter Brooks have long seen in melodramatic narratives.[40]

Romance and the Love Story

Philipp enters the film directly after the title frame, heading out of his apartment building before bicycling to work at a school. These shots (fig. 5) establish Philipp's location and further situate the film in late 1980s Berlin, while delivering the first of twin sequences at the start and end of the film. Philipp soon introduces himself at

Figure 5. Philipp bicycles to work, appearing, like Matthias in the ambulance, in crowded East Berlin.

the front of a classroom of high-school students, before writing his name on the chalkboard. There is some tittering among the students in the classroom, but this is the start of what Philipp hopes will be a different kind of teacher-student relationship. He is young—about twenty-seven years old, according to notes in the script—and wants to be an unconventional teacher in his interactions and assignments.[41] The depiction of Philipp's teaching style endears him to the viewer while it also illustrates yet another contrast between him and the social structure around him. Not only is Philipp younger than other authority figures at the school (except for Tanja), but he also represents a clear deviation from the stern, tired senior teachers and principal. GDR society as depicted in the film becomes a contrast between youthful energy and aging authority structures. Philipp's own surname is another indication of his role in the narrative, marking him as a kind of ironic allegory: "Klahrmann" (including the German word for "clear" but with an unusual spelling) turns out to be misleading, since his identity and position in *Coming Out* are anything but clear.

After Philipp's class, we witness via tracking and stationary shots an awkward meeting between him and his teacher colleague Tanja, making her first appearance, as they collide in the school's stairwell, Tanja having been obscured to Philipp by two students carrying a bulletin board. A medium shot shows Philipp and Tanja in the stairwell after they regain their footing (fig. 6). Tanja has a bloody nose, so Philipp leads her to the women's restroom. In front of a line of toilet stalls, Philipp tries to help stanch the bleeding. He brings Tanja a hand towel, which she then asks him to wet with water. Once he brings it back to her, she complains, "It's too wet!" When a female student emerges from one of the stalls and walks obliviously between Tanja and Philipp, Philipp says, "I'm so embarrassed." "I'll be okay," Tanja manages to say. The humor of this sequence arises from contradiction and diverging expectations. From Philipp's calm departure from his class and walk down the hallway, we progress to a shot that gives us an inkling that a collision may be coming. Both the viewer's foreknowledge and the crash itself are comedic devices. Following the two characters' impact, the film delivers a series of punctuated, awkwardly comedic elements: the yelp that Tanja releases, her bloody nose, their exit to the restroom, Philipp's visible discomfort and embarrassment, Tanja's annoyance at his incorrect wetting of the towel, and the student's flushing of the toilet and obliviousness in walking between Tanja and Philipp. All create a moment that potentially sets up expectations for a storyline resembling a romantic comedy.

In bringing Philipp and Tanja together in this manner, the film accomplishes some queerly critical work. It also follows what one might expect from romantic or screwball comedy (which *Coming Out* is not), both of which are forms that rely on establishing, challenging, and then restoring order. A stock comedic device is the establishment of its story trajectory in earnest after establishing a (cisheterosexual) romantic couple, whose successes and failures help to determine the comedic or tragic nature of the story.[42] Writing

Figure 6. A chance meeting, a device common in romantic comedies, here in the form of a collision, introduces Tanja to Philipp and the viewer.

about slapstick, a comedic tool that has been used in many genres including romantic and screwball comedies, Tom Gunning observes that comedic devices often change the trajectory of a narrative or alter the audience's expectations of a character by "detouring, if not derailing" "the apparent predictability of an action or system"[43] *Coming Out*'s use of this mechanism sets up the expectation in the viewer not only that the two characters will become romantically involved but also that their relationship will be successful and could in fact be an important part of the ordered structure of the narrative, as one might expect from a romantic story. Tamar Jeffers McDonald's defining criterion for the romantic comedy is its focus on "a quest for love, which portrays this quest in a light-hearted way and almost always [leads it] to a successful conclusion."[44] As one finds out later in the film, Philipp's relationship with Tanja destroys the ordered life he had made by suppressing his own identity and denying the reality of past events and his own deeper feelings. Philipp becomes a component of a formula whose presence will allow for its disruption. The film has now introduced three of the most important characters, populating the "love triangle" I mentioned above. Matthias will soon join the triad when Philipp is inspired to explore his identity. Philipp and Tanja are now connected by what has already unfolded. The viewer's expectation of a link between them in the ensuing plot has been established.

Philipp and Tanja's Courtship

The film proceeds to develop the relationship between Tanja and Philipp. The scene after the stairwell collision and Philipp's nursing of Tanja's bloody nose shows the two on a date. After they dance, Philipp orders two rounds of a strong drink for each of them. Tanja excuses herself, looking like she might be sick. Next to their spot at the bar sit another woman and man on a date (fig. 7). Another comedic element introduces this couple: we hear the woman speaking before the camera pans to the right to see them, as the woman recalls that the two had first met at the optician, when the man stepped on her contact lens. The woman keeps her male companion, her "little angel," from drinking wine, suggesting that he stick to mineral water. She effusively tells him that his glasses make him look so much better than he does without them and make him look so handsome and manly. After the two kiss, slightly sheepishly, Tanja returns to the bar. Her face is now covered in makeup, and her hair is teased and hair-sprayed into a large arrangement (fig. 8). "Now let's party!" she says after taking another sip of her drink.

The nervous couple at the bar invites the viewer to compare what is currently being shown to what has just been shown and what follows. This sequence is one of contrasting or ironic moments, of which there are several in *Coming Out*. The shots that follow of Tanja and Philipp dancing are unsurprising; the conversation they have at the bar proceeds along similarly predictable lines, slightly awkward and plausible for a first date. Tanja's possible nausea and temporary exit from the scene also gesture toward the comedic, even more so given

Figure 7. A couple next to Tanja and Philipp at the bar have a humorously awkward first date, serving as comparison and contrast.

Figure 8. Tanja appears after making herself over in the restroom, adding to the slight awkwardness of their date.

the way Manzel plays it, using subtle changes in facial expression. The collision in the school stairwell established a structural, narrative expectation for the two characters' future trajectory. Following that conventional path, Tanja and Philipp might end up like the nameless couple at the bar; those two characters, too, began their relationship with a comedic event. Instead, both Tanja and Philipp are performing something here: Tanja gets rather drunk, which she says is unusual, and Philipp plays the attentive future boyfriend. Here, *Coming Out* delivers one of the first of multiple examples of pantomime, a performance made up of prescribed gestures and stock characters. Tanja and Philipp enact and display various layers of meaning, while obscuring others.

After a transitional scene that shows Tanja and Philipp walking back to her apartment, the viewer sees Philipp standing in her living room, leading to their first romantic encounter. Tanja encourages Philipp to stay, offers him tea, takes his coat—all friendly and accommodating gestures, while also detached. As the two talk in Tanja's apartment, the viewer learns more about the characters' history, including their prior interactions. Contrary to Philipp's assertion that they have never socialized before, Tanja corrects him and says that they danced together at a university party. She tells Philipp that "all the girls liked [him]" and "everyone knew" that he had a thing going with one girl. When Philipp begins to ask about the tea, Tanja interrupts him and says abruptly, "I still like you," before leaving to start the tea in the adjacent kitchen. Philipp joins her in the doorway to the kitchen, where they kiss, before the film cuts to a shot of the two of them sitting in bed drinking sparkling wine. Tanja suggests that they throw the glasses over their shoulders, like people such as the actress Romy Schneider (1938–82) do "in the movies." Tanja is completely infatuated. Philipp asks if she would want him as a boyfriend, to which Tanja responds by throwing her glass over her shoulder and embracing him. "And I thought . . . My God," she says, relieved.

With its invoking of stereotypical motifs of excess (like intoxicating romance, drunken stars, tossed glasses), this bedroom scene puts Tanja and Philipp into the fast-moving current of a heterosexual love story. The wider shot of Tanja's bedroom (fig. 9)

Figure 9. Philipp plays a role in a conventional heterosexual romance.

reveals on her wall a poster for *Guten Morgen, Du Schöne* (*Good Morning, My Lovely*, directed by Thomas Langhoff), the episodic GDR television adaptation of its namesake, Maxie Wander's 1977 book of narrativized interviews with East German women. Both the book and the episodes, and the movie poster pointed toward the hidden expectations of women in society. Ironically for what will take place in the plot, the film leads one to believe that Tanja's position has a favorable outlook, but the reference to Wander's work is a reminder that women still face obstacles.

These scenes establish one of the two primary romantic relationships in *Coming Out*, in so doing building expectations for a heterosexual romantic storyline. They also take the characters to another height of emotional expression, as Tanja explicitly says they should emulate "the movies," yet another mimicry, both of a typical love story and the roles that appear in one. Romantic comedies or relationship films usually feature cues that mark the work as belonging to this genre. These include showing characters that offer a contrast to the appropriate partner for the protagonist and repeating motifs of love and marriage (using props like beds, candlelight, and flowers, for example). Tropes and genre devices used in romantic comedy include the pratfall, slapstick, breakup and reconciliation, and masquerade, just to name a few that appear, even if in queered form, in *Coming Out*.[45] Many viewers are familiar with the most common formula of romantic comedies: "boy meets, loses, regains girl."[46] So far, *Coming Out* has set in motion the "boy meets girl" narrative, encouraging the viewer to imagine the story along those predictable lines. One underlying assumption behind these stories' structure is the primacy of monogamy and the linked outcome of conventional marriage.[47]

The predictability of genre raises questions of structural expectations, beyond those of the viewer. As Kyle Stevens has argued, the predictability of the romantic comedy genre and its successful execution depend upon a privileged position within a structural framework: in this case, cisheterosexuality and its narratives have primacy in media production. The genre's codependency on cisheterosexuality is required both to be able to produce iterations of the genre and to be able to view those iterations as successful.[48] Conventionally predictable genres like romantic relationship films carry the imprimatur of the norm. One reason that this genre is the most derided by cishet critics and adored by, for example, many queer viewers, Stevens argues, is that the critics await narrative and genre deviation from their own privileged, everyday experience, in which happy endings following a well-worn path are still possible.[49] Queer viewers, according to Stevens, because they are structurally inhibited from experiencing them, find novelty and joy in such happy endings.

In a film about homosexuality, or specifically gay men, one could expect there to be deviations from the usual heterosexual trajectory in the narrative pattern of the romantic genre. Such differences do appear in the film's story, as Philipp maneuvers in the complex field of his feelings, relationships, and responsibilities. Here, *Coming Out* shares some traits with the "radical romantic comedy," Hollywood films that were not as committed to ensuring a happy ending or at least firmly establishing a couple (for instance, Mike Nichols's 1967 film *The Graduate*).[50] DEFA, too, had comedies that deviated from the conventional pattern, like Peter Kahane's film *Ete und Ali* (*Ete and Ali*, 1984). Yet, *Coming Out*, though not a comedy, is still best understood as a melodramatic queering of the love story. With the film's repeated turns to devices of romantic comedies, one could forget the opening scenes showing the consequences of Matthias's desperate suicide attempt. Even at the point in the film when Tanja and Philipp are established as a couple, Matthias is a lingering reminder of a social reality that seems alien to developing cishet bliss.

Beyond establishing some romantic structure and laying a foundation of Tanja and Philipp's relationship, however, the scenes of their initial coupling provide hints about Philipp's background. The two did know each other previously, within relatively recent memory. More intriguing, though, is the fact that in these scenes Tanja uses a recurring device both in the film and in discourses of gender and sexuality: gossip or "common knowledge," which adds to our understanding of social expectations and the possibility of public scrutiny. The viewer learns about what "all the girls" thought about Philipp, although this could be a way of covering up what Tanja herself thought about him. Her utterance of "And I thought ... My God" after Philipp asks if she would have him as her boyfriend similarly points to hidden information about him and sets up more of the story.

This is our first glimpse of the structure of expectations in both the world of the film and the real world beyond it. As discussed above, even *Coming Out*'s title signals to the viewer that the workings of the "closet" (and how one might come out of it) will relate to, if not determine, the story's conclusion. What Tanja implies is that there is an open secret about Philipp, which judges him according to the dominant structure of heteronormative expectations. The underlying secret, which Tanja suggests has circulated in rumors, is the possibility that Philipp has queer desires. It is both typical and tragic that others around Philipp might know more about aspects of his personality than he does himself. Jack Halberstam has astutely observed that "self-knowledge is the secret kept by society" from the homosexual.[51]

Now that Tanja and Philipp are established as a couple, the film can proceed toward developments that will reveal the story's conflict. The subsequent scene shows Philipp relaxed and serene. We see him dancing in a hora with his students in the high-school classroom. The students are clearly enjoying themselves, laughing and cheering. Their happiness deflates when the classroom door abruptly opens and the school's stern principal (Gertraud Kreißig) enters the room. The music stops, and Philipp and the principal stare at each other in alternating close-up shots—a standoff. Philipp opens the folded chalkboard to reveal an essay assignment, much to the disappointment of the students. Once Philipp returns to a more traditional teaching posture, the principal relents and leaves the room. On the chalkboard, we see a poem by Bertolt Brecht, which Philipp proceeds to recite. Brecht's poem from around 1955, which begins "I need no headstone," thematizes the use of a life and of remembering one. One interpretation of the poem sees the text as a Marxist challenge to critically examine the contributions of others in order to improve society.[52] Philipp asks the students in an essay prompt, "What moves me as I read this poem? What will I move after reading this poem?" Like Brecht's understated exhortation to think creatively ("He made suggestions. We / accepted them."),[53] Philipp's demeanor and this assignment mark a desire for improvement through social involvement.

This scene illustrates tension between generations and ideologies. The abrupt entry of the principal and her disapproving visage ends the joy that had filled Philipp's classroom. This encounter with the school's administration marks Philipp as unconventional at best and an outsider at worst. It is not coincidental that Philipp is a teacher in this story. In *Epistemology of the Closet*, Sedgwick discusses the fraught position of gay teachers, who face a dilemma in both demands for disclosure and the interpretation that their personal reality is toxic to the environment in which they work. She writes that "the space for simply existing as a gay person who is a teacher is in fact bayonetted through and through, from both sides, by the vectors of a disclosure at once compulsory and forbidden."[54] There is great significance in Philipp's being a *gay* teacher but also in his position as a teacher in and of itself. The implications of the former will become clearer toward the end of the film. The latter—the role of a teacher and how it relates to what is happening in the film and in the society it depicts—begins to be important at this point.

Signaling usefulness and marking generational tension become the background for Philipp's deepening relationship with Tanja. There are shots of Philipp bringing some of his belongings out of his high-rise apartment building and putting them in a cart to move to Tanja's apartment, among them a paper jumping-jack toy (a *Hampelmann*), which will reappear later. The recurring association of Philipp with the toy is not a positive one. In colloquial German the term for this toy can refer to an individual who is either easily manipulated or cannot make their own decisions. Another shot pans and follows Philipp as he pushes his cart across a street intersection. Gray, worn buildings form the backdrop for these scenes, linking to what we see soon on a stage. Before a cut, while Philipp is still pushing his cart, music begins and forms a bridge into the next scene. The music is from Mozart's *The Magic Flute* (1791), performed by the Komische Oper in Berlin. Onstage, in front of a set that resembles the gray facades from the previous shot, a man and a woman sing a duet. Philipp is at the performance with some of his students. Adding a surprising and awkward component to the concert scene, one student sitting next to Philipp, Irina (Cornelia Schirmer), puts her hand on Philipp's thigh after rebuffing a display of affection from a young man behind her. This occurs at one of the climaxes of the duet.

Most of *The Magic Flute*'s wild story has nothing to do with *Coming Out*. The choice of this moment in the opera, however, and of this staging, is meaningful. Two of the opera's characters, Papageno (Andreas David) and Papagena (Barbara Dollfus), have spotted each other after being separated. Papageno, a bird-catcher, had seen Papagena first as an old crone, but she had turned into a beautiful young woman after he agreed to marry her. She was spirited away, leaving Papageno distraught. He tried to find Papagena and summon her back but to no avail. Their famous stammering duet in Act 2 ("Pa-Pa-Pa-Pa-Papagena!") begins as Papageno sees Papagena. The lyrics are an ode to marital domesticity and heterosexual procreation, as the pair sings about belonging to each other and having row upon row of children: little Papagenos and Papagenas.

This part of the film is preoccupied with Philipp's developing relationship with Tanja, in addition to its highlighting of social problems in East Germany. What happens on the opera stage, while also being another of the film's pantomimes, serves as an ironic contrast and a commentary on the diegesis. Is this to be Philipp's future, or, as it were, is the joke on Philipp? A geometric romantic comedy of errors is also visible in the theater seats, as Philipp's student Irina rejects her boyfriend's affections in favor of her advance on Philipp, who sits next to another student, Lutz (Robert Hummel) (not yet known to be gay but later to be coupled with Matthias), all while Philipp and the others watch a dramatic enactment of cishet, marital, procreative joy. This moment is one clue among many that Philipp is out of place and has not yet found his footing in the cisheteronormative world around him. It is not just the operatic marital bliss onstage that reminds one of the ongoing plot. Beyond what we see of the opera in the film, some of this staging's portrayal of *The Magic Flute* clearly resembles the world of the contemporaneous GDR.

The procreative joy about which Papageno and Papagena sing carries over into the following sequence, which is remarkable for its depiction of another social ill of the GDR: specifically far-right racism and violence. The scene begins with a close-up on Philipp's face as he and his students ride the subway following the performance. Activity in the car catches his attention, and the music ends (fig. 10). Three young skinheads are harassing and assaulting a Black man (Pierre Sanoussi-Bliss), referred to in the script as an "Arab man."[55] Shots show passengers around the car either ignoring or watching without intervening as these three white men attack. Philipp stands up, breaks up the assault, and becomes the new target. Some of Philipp's students get involved, yelling at and pushing the skinheads. A shot shows that the subway stops at Marx-Engels-Platz, and the skinheads run out of the car. A brief subsequent shot shows Philipp and his students walking away from the station, while he holds tissues to his bleeding nose and face. Lutz and Irina jockey for Philipp's attention and the position of the one comforting him.

Right-wing extremism was one form of youth rebellion and disruption in East Germany. Antifascism had been a stated goal of governmental policy and ideology since the nation's founding

Figure 10. Skinheads assault a Black man in a subway car, prompting Philipp's intervention.

in 1949. Youth subcultures expanded into left- and right-wing extremism as an expression of "radical alienation" from the GDR's ruling party. This alienation was both a symptom and contributing factor in what became the disintegration of "real-existing socialism," the form of society and economy in the GDR.[56] Beyond this youth disillusionment, however, there was a real, more complex problem of developing far-right extremism. The GDR's official policies of antifascism had resulted in suppression, rather than a complete elimination, of far-right ideologies.[57] Amid the turbulence of 1989, neo-Nazi activity increased more rapidly. In the years following the opening of the GDR's borders that year, the country's collapse, and German unification in 1990, racist violence became even worse, reaching new extremes. Black American lesbian poet Audre Lorde (1934–92), who had spent much time on various trips to Germany starting in 1984, wrote in her poem "East Berlin" (1993), "It feels dangerous now / to be Black in Berlin."[58] While they were not the only attacks, the worst incidents of racist and xenophobic violence in Hoyerswerda (1991), Rostock (1992), Mölln (1992), and Solingen (1993) became symbols for the extremist terror carried out in the years following German unification. The inclusion of the skinheads' assault and Philipp's intervention serve the dual purpose of reminding the audience of the existence of such problems in the GDR and of the possibility of effecting change in society.[59]

The possibility for change is called into question, however, when Philipp later scolds his students for their work on the essay topic inspired by Brecht's poem. "How are you going to improve things in the future?" Philipp asks, clearly disappointed. "You're all so bright, and you write this boring, tired, and well-behaved junk.... How are you going to fight stupidity in the world?" This scene comes immediately after Philipp had been active in making a change in his environment, moving to break up the skinheads' assault and to protect the victim. The black eye we see on Philipp's face is a reminder of the engagement he is demanding of his students. Here, too, *Coming Out* clearly provides commentary on the social circumstances in which it was being produced.

Once again, though, the film takes us back to the reality of Philipp's developing and ongoing relationship with Tanja. Especially in this part of the film, the two threads form a counterpoint: Philipp's brave social action, his individuality, and the scolding of his students for their social conformity precede more-domestic scenes. In Tanja's kitchen, Philipp tells her that he will be going to visit his mother. Tanja is unable to come along because, she says, her friend "Redford is coming by" to stay and meet Philipp and see if he's good enough for her. Philipp doesn't know it yet, but this is a sign of trouble. Philipp is temporarily diverted from going to see his mother when he and Tanja have sex, after which a comedic shot shows Tanja munching on pickles as she gazes at Philipp's naked body while he sleeps (fig. 11). Philipp must rush to his mother's, running along a street while holding a bouquet of flowers. Shortly after the scene starts, as he gets closer to his family's home, a children's song begins to play, marking

Figure 11. With its suggestive use of pickles, a humorous shot shows Tanja's success in delaying Philipp's departure to see his mother.

for the audience where Philipp is headed: back to a position of being a child and playing the dutiful son.

Philipp's return to his family home and the conversation with his mother reveal more about the common perception of him. When he arrives, the camera pans to reveal his mother (Walfriede Schmitt) hunched over her work papers, asleep. She awakens surly, complaining that he has not been around to help with household chores like before. "I was a child," Philipp says. "I lived here." Both seem defeated by the conversation and what it reveals about their relationship, before Philipp makes a disclosure of his own: he puts a photo in front of his mother (fig. 12). "That's her," Philipp says. "My girlfriend." "You have a girlfriend?" she asks incredulously. Still perplexed, she moves on and asks Philipp to wash the dishes and do the laundry. She starts typing on a typewriter, shaking her head and still saying with shock, "Isn't that something?" As before, this scene between Philipp and his mother reveals common knowledge about Philipp: specifically, his mother's suspicion that he was gay, as revealed by her ongoing confusion at his coupling with a woman. The characters' interaction shows their strained relationship, too. Fitting for a melodrama, one is reminded that others' perception of Philipp is outside of his control. His motivation for telling his mother about his relationship with Tanja is another attempt to conform to the many expectations of those around him, including his family and society.

Queer Exploration

Although Philipp's relationship with his mother is not ideal, his life by now is stable. The film has shown Philipp's developing relationship with Tanja. Professionally, Philipp is possibly a loose cannon from the establishment's perspective, but that benefits his reputation with his adoring students. But his world loses its stability as he comes home to Tanja's apartment. We see Philipp's jumping-

Figure 12. Philipp's news of his romance with Tanja puzzles his mother, with whom he has a difficult relationship.

Figure 13. The toy on the door signals Philipp's lack of control, especially in this scene when he becomes reacquainted with Jakob.

jack toy from earlier, now shown in Tanja's apartment in a shot of the apartment door through which Philipp enters (fig. 13). The toy hangs on the inside of the door, standing as a reminder of Philipp's childhood while also representing Philipp himself: an object to be manipulated, even by his own misunderstanding of his desires; not fully a self-determining individual. The next several minutes of the film are some of the most consequential for Philipp's trajectory as a character and for the development of the story.

After Philipp returns to Tanja's apartment and begins making something in the kitchen, "Redford" spots Philipp. Redford is Tanja's nickname for her friend Jakob (Axel Wandtke). When he sees Philipp, they are both surprised. The sudden inclusion of composer (and the director's son) Stefan Carow's dramatic nondiegetic music signals a disruption that complements the camerawork and editing—all contribute to the melodramatic meeting. Tanja enters the kitchen and asks, "Do you know each other?" Philipp is still stunned and unable to fully answer, "We were ..." "... classmates," Jakob says. After a cut, Tanja and Jakob are having a good time, but Philipp is still visibly shocked and not participating in the conversation. He abruptly leaves the room, and we see him in the bathroom running water over his head. The camera closes in on him as he rises from the bathtub and is surrounded by a jungle of hanging women's undergarments. The camera gets close and moves to the left to see him gaze at himself, stricken, in the bathroom mirror (fig. 14), his visage split by the mirror's panels. While the reason is still unknown to the viewer, Philipp is in a crisis. The music, editing, and camerawork, combined with Philipp's distress, communicate an uncomfortable agitation.

Philipp returns, and the awkwardness remains. As Jakob departs, we see Tanja's front door again, the jumping-jack toy again in prominent position, centered in the shot, staring at the viewer. Before leaving, Jakob pauses in the threshold and says to Philipp, "I guess you didn't get my letters? ... It's not important. Bye." Tanja is annoyed and asks Philipp what his problem is. He responds by quickly and forcefully kissing and embracing her. The dramatic music returns and again signals a disruption. The guitar, flute, and cello interweave in an off-putting frenzy and overlap with the following scene. Jakob

Figure 14. After Jakob's appearance in the prior scene, the segmented mirror captures Philipp's distress and the collision of his prior and current lives.

and Philipp's past has become a momentarily puzzling plot point for the viewer. Delaying its resolution, the narrative temporarily resides in the tension prompted by Jakob's arrival—an event that seems to have great significance for both Jakob and Philipp.

The film's original treatment (that is, the draft script without camera directions) and earlier versions of the screenplay include much more detail about these two characters' past history with one another.[60] In the opening of a later screenplay set for filming, there is a scene with Philipp and Jakob, approximately sixteen years old, wrestling in a school gym, eventually going too far and having to be broken up by a teacher, followed by a common trope in schoolboy dramas: a shower scene. Here, Philipp and Jakob are alone in the communal shower. Their play with the shower water leads to an erotic moment, which the gym teacher witnesses in shock but does not interrupt.[61] This leads to a sense of crisis in Philipp's home, as shown in the following scene. His parents are embarrassed, having been told about "a certain incident in the gymnasium—in the shower."[62] The way this scene is conceived features repeated close-up shots, focusing on the reactions of the individuals involved, as the parents try to overcome their discomfort. Philipp's parents lecture him (his father even hits him), telling him that he is their hope for the future and is in danger of ruining everything for himself and for them. The scene ends with Philipp dejected and crying, alone.[63]

It is not clear whether this material was ever filmed. The camera shots described often position Philipp as an isolated figure, whether in his family apartment, on a subway platform, or even in scenes on Alexanderplatz. He remains socially disconnected, either ignoring people or seemingly unaware of their presence.[64] As with the other planned scenes, the effect was meant to be achieved through close-ups of Philipp and medium-long and long shots usually placing him as a centrally isolated figure. Such sequences could have provided greater context for Philipp's development as a character. Beyond adding to the melodrama, the sequences would have made more obvious the familial and societal pressure on Philipp to conform to gender and sexual expectations. The script versions show that one of the filmmakers' intentions was to illustrate Philipp's severe emotional isolation. Absent the exposition provided by the youthful episode, the viewer is left to infer the cause of Philipp's unease.

Moving back to the scene with Jakob that did make it into the film, however, the encounter with Jakob has shaken Philipp. In a brief transitional scene with teacher colleague Frau Möllemann (Gudrun Ritter), his expression remains vacant and immobile. She speaks about what she feels is Philipp's current problem: his difficulties as a young, new teacher. Her attempt at comforting Philipp reveals something about the social and professional world in which he finds himself and will experience his coming out: that it is stressful, characterized by challenges that students pose and plagued by the gossipy judgments of one's colleagues. There are at least two ways to interpret Frau Möllemann's comments: they could be general, based mostly on her own personal experience, or they could be advance notice to Philipp about discussions of him that may already be ongoing. The conversation is likely a combination of the two, based on the administrative discipline he faces later in the film. This scene functions as an echo of the previous emotional upheaval caused for Philipp by Jakob's reappearance in his life.

Philipp becomes despondent and begins to drink; the viewer sees him walking on a sidewalk, holding a large bottle of liquor. This next sequence that follows both Jakob's unexpected arrival and the shock Philipp shows with Frau Möllemann is one of the most important in *Coming Out*. Its value comes from both its function in the film's story and its landmark quality in (GDR) film history. For the first time, an East German feature film took the viewer into a gay bar and showed a version of what happens there and the people who go there. The short documentary, *The Other Love* (1988), had also revealed some aspects of LGBTQ+ life in East Germany, but in documentary form and in a more limited release than *Coming Out* was to have. Otherwise there had been little open and positive portrayal of homosexuals in East German media. Carow cast people from the East Berlin gay scene for the film's depiction of LGBTQ+ life (some of whom, including Dirk Kummer [Matthias], appeared in *The Other Love*). Both bars used as locations in *Coming Out* (Zum Burgfrieden and Die Schoppenstube) were actual gay bars and two of the more popular spots in the divided city's gay scene.

The camera captures Philipp's drunken approach, highlighting the explosion of color in the window of the bar and through the panes of glass in its entrance door. It is a different world inside. The colors (visible through the door in fig. 15), mark a contrast with the gray and muted tones of the buildings, characteristic of much of the film's external world. Philipp is pulled into the bar by a group of patrons in costume (fig. 15) and into a costume party, which adds to the spectacular nature of the queer world to which the viewer and Philipp are introduced.

The sequence upon entering the bar is deliberately overwhelming. Unlike much of what has been on-screen before, this series of shots

Figure 15. Philipp is pulled from the gray normal outside into the colorful world of the gay bar.

highlights the wide range of individuals found inside, augmented by the various costumes, drag, exposed buttocks, hairstyles, makeup, sequins, feathers, and dancing, while Frank Schöbel's song "Gold in Your Eyes" plays. Famed trans icon Charlotte von Mahlsdorf (1928–2002), who hosted meetings of the GDR's first gay-rights group in the nineteenth-century museum she ran, appears as a barmaid and soon tells Philipp her own gender-sexual origin story (fig. 16).[65] The music in the bar is mostly *Schlager*, the stereotypical German popular music that disarms with its schmaltzy, sentimental lyrics and instrumentation. In this way, the music we hear during the bar scene, which is set during a costume party for Carnival, differs from the original film music, the tonally and rhythmically complex work by Stefan Carow. It is in this sequence that Matthias first spies Philipp. Matthias, appearing as a Pierrot clown (a pantomime character) with a whitened face and a tulle collar around his neck (fig. 17), later helps Walter, the older bar patron, to bring an intoxicated Philipp home. Beyond the visual stimulation of this sequence, the music contributes to an emotional ride for the audience, with highs and lows corresponding to alternating moments of happy music and dancing

Figure 16. A link to East German (and earlier) queer history, Charlotte von Mahlsdorf as a barmaid puts Philipp more at ease in the bar.

Figure 17. Matthias as a sad clown, evoking Pierrot and his unrequited love.

and a moment of sadness, when the camera and the downbeat music emphasize the isolation of the random partygoers caught on-screen. Shortly after Philipp is dragged into the establishment, the waiter, Achim (Michael Gwisdek), finds a spot for Philipp at the bar. Achim addresses Philipp, just to the side of the camera. "You don't need to be afraid. Everyone starts out this way," Achim says. "Be brave." In this poignant moment, Achim addresses Philipp as well as many viewers of the film.

The ordinariness of what is otherwise unusual is another element of this sequence. The camera observes Philipp at the bar accepting a drink from the emcee before he turns to eavesdrop on a conversation one hears clearly over the music. A baritone drag queen, identified in the script as Egbert (Dieter Okras), complains about a toothache before also grumbling that her partner, Hartmut (whom she refers to as "her highness"), isn't helping with construction of their new house. A conversation Egbert has with two other bargoers is revealing of the variety of professions represented at the bar: among them are teachers, a child psychologist, and a construction machinist.

Some viewers and critics disapproved of the way Carow showed the gay bar scene. The camera first introduces viewers to a kaleidoscopic cornucopia of queerness, which was criticized for being overdone. Journalist Ilona Rühmann, for example, opined that Carow includes "every possible prejudiced cliché" in this sequence.[66] Henryk Goldberg wrote of Carow's "exoticist" approach to showing homosexuality in the GDR context.[67] It is appropriate for Philipp's situation that one enters the bar as if it were something completely foreign, since this is the case both for the main character and many in the audience. Already in the expert opinions supporting the film's production, there were questions about how much the film should try to manage the audience's expectations as it depicted the life of queer people. The experts, Carow, and Witt hoped for a film whose portrayal would not be too positive, negative, or stereotypical.

These several minutes make a truly remarkable sequence. The music, the costumes, the queer affection, the visual stimulation—all of it astonishes and overwhelms. Carow knew that this would be a remarkable moment for the film's story, for the viewers, and for the history of GDR film. The impulse to make the film was for

Carow not primarily about breaking a taboo and forcing people to see something that they had not previously observed; telling a love story was more important.[68] In an interview circulated by the DEFA Studios export branch as press material, Carow describes how an individual needs love to develop. Carow knew that the tolerance of homosexuality in any society, especially East Germany, would be contingent on gradual change. On the one hand, *Coming Out*, taken as a whole, is an example of the slower approach to tolerance. On the other hand, the entry into the gay club explodes the idea of slow progress and is fitting for Carow's use of melodrama to tell a queer story. Like the film itself, which benefits from its sampling of genre devices and filmic modes, Philipp's first foray into the gay scene combines reality and artifice, professional actors and amateurs, all filmed not on a set but in an authentic headquarters of queerness.

But this carnivalesque sequence must soon come to an end. Philipp is not yet ready to become one of the bar's regulars: he cannot yet accept his own queerness. He has been drinking and enjoying himself, smiling and laughing in a brief montage of him at the bar and other shots around the space, including the emcee's flirting with him. A drag queen approaches the bar and flirts with Philipp, too. He reacts badly, pushing her away and struggling before falling, drunk, to the floor and exclaiming, "What do you all want from me? I have nothing to . . . !" Annemarie, the only lesbian highlighted in the film (Gudrun Okras, fig. 18), disappointedly finishes his sentence: "'I have nothing to do with you,' he wanted to say." Matthias and Walter then take Philipp back to his apartment and deposit him there.

True to the film's melodramatic intentions, the bar sequence displays a range of emotional highs and lows. If we think back to the conventions of melodrama, we find the (cishet) love story and its all-important triangular relationship. Matthias's arrival and connection to Philipp in this scene completes the triangle, although that has not yet been completely revealed. Not much time has elapsed since Philipp saw Jakob again at Tanja's after so long, but in that short

Figure 18. Annemarie sees through Philipp's drunkenness to his discomfort and fear.

time the world he has constructed has begun to fall apart. The past has reemerged and taken primacy over the present, a facade, that Philipp had created with Tanja. Philipp must now be terrified about the consequences of this resurgence of his past.

Change and Upheaval

Having briefly experienced Berlin's queer subculture, Philipp is now on a path toward radical transformation of his life. He visits Jakob at his apartment, an occasion that dredges up more emotional wreckage from the past. Philipp joins Jakob and his unnamed partner (Holger Siemann) for mulled wine, and Jakob tells the partner that he and Philipp went to school together. The conversation upsets Jakob and leads to the revelation that Philipp's parents tried to buy off Jakob with a bicycle and a compass to keep him away from their son. As Jakob starts to explain that he had to accept because his family was poor, Philipp quickly leaves.

Jakob's unexpected reemergence in Philipp's life has set much in motion. Since then, multiple situations have shown Philipp coming face to face with what could be his new reality as a gay man, whether that be the nightlife of the clubs or a same-sex partnership and life at home. Last in a line of these glimpses is a brief scene, directly following Philipp's flight from Jakob's apartment, in which he walks through a subway station. The recurring tremulous music provides an accompaniment to Philipp's entrance. The music's volume subsides as we hear a man off-screen shout "Hey, faggot!" Because all one sees on the screen is a full-length shot of Philipp, the source of this yelled slur is unknown. It could be directed at Philipp, but it becomes clear that he is not the target. Matching Philipp's glance, the camera cuts to a shot of a young man standing alone at the intersection of station hallways. This individual's appearance—dyed blond hair with purple accents, vibrant pink scarf, earring—has captured the attention of a group of three men, who approach and then attack him (fig. 19). Philipp's face reveals his horror: the shock of the assault combined with the likely fear that he may be next. We can imagine that Philipp sees the attack as a glimpse of his own fate. Unlike the earlier incident in which he and his students witnessed skinheads

Figure 19. The view as Philipp witnesses an antiqueer attack.

attacking a Black man and Philipp tried to intervene, this time he flees. As he slows down, the camera captures his fright and shame in the form of his defeated retreat through the staircase railing (fig. 20). Philipp has become uncertain and timid.

In its usual pattern, the film transitions back to Philipp's other (primary) life, that of professional obligations, teaching, his students, and Tanja. The camera cuts to a youth club, the kind that, starting in the 1970s, the GDR government began to allow as a way for young people to organize their own leisure time within certain parameters. We see Lutz backed by a small group of musicians (drums, horn, bass, and guitar). The club is packed beyond capacity (fig. 21). Lutz announces a number called "Song from the Ghetto," which has a klezmer feel and moves from a melancholic start to an agitated and upbeat coda. A cutaway shot shows Philipp and Tanja in the audience, sitting among many young people. All look toward Lutz with rapt attention. While Lutz sings (he is lip-synching to a vocal recorded by Karsten Troyke[69]), the handheld camera passes through the crowded audience before it reaches a view of Lutz and the band.

Figure 20. Like an unseen observer, the camera watches Philipp's flight from the scene of the queer bashing.

Figure 21. After the scene of antiqueer violence, we see a packed youth club where Lutz sings about belonging and familial bonds.

The poem that forms the basis of the song's lyrics is "When Nobody Calls Me" by the Russian-born, Yiddish-speaking poet Kadya Molodowsky (1894–1975). Yiddish poetry scholar Kathryn Hellerstein writes that "Molodowsky's poems reshape the questions that pervaded modern Yiddish poetry: questions about the poet's political responsibility, national identity, religious belief, aestheticism, and individualism."[70] "When Nobody Calls Me" comes from a collection, *In the Land of My Bones*, published in 1937, two years after Molodowsky and her husband emigrated from Poland to the United States. Experiences of exile and belonging spring forth from the poem:

> My mother does not call me by name—
> Because my mother is dead.
> My father does not call me by name—
> Because my father is gone.
> And God does not call me by name—
> Because God plays at a Purim masquerade,
> He's disguised himself as a dog

And mourns loudly in the night.
I beat him off with a stick
To make him leave me alone.

Rest, my heart—
Rest a moment while God is away.
Rest a moment
While my body is drawn out with patience.
Rest a moment
Until a bell peals,
Until the mourning that hangs
Like a sack on my back calls.
Rest a moment—
One moment without God.[71]

Molodowsky's original poem, from which the lyrics of Lutz's song are excerpted, conveys a distinct sense of isolation and adaptation. The poem's narrator is removed from their parents by both death and geography. God, too, is distant, not calling them by name and engaging in an act of deceptive manipulation. The speaker must counter God's unwelcome vocalizations, is driven to seek respite, and is mournfully disconnected from familial or personal bonds.

The position of Jewishness within East Germany was controversial. It is important to consider this question in the context of the GDR's history of espousing antifascism while also suppressing minority identity. The philosophies undergirding GDR self-identifications of antifascism and socialism stymied efforts to highlight the experiences of most persecuted groups. The GDR frequently obscured specific questions of identity, including most prominently, but not only, Jewishness, with respect to memory of the Holocaust.[72] The prevailing conception of a Marxist-Leninist state demanded a unity of purpose and group identity, diminishing any self-identifications beyond every citizen's expected socialist commitment. Individuals could face social and governmental pressure if they refused to stop asserting their Jewish identity; the anti-identitarian drive of the regime also conflated—especially in the GDR's first thirty years—Jewishness and the GDR's imperialist, capitalist foes.[73]

As at other points in *Coming Out*, the construction of this scene—the layers of music, the lyrics, cultural connections beyond the edges of the frame—conveys more cultural content than is at first apparent. Here, Lutz's performance and the associated spectacle are compelling evidence of a vibrant youth culture. The song, with its themes of overcoming challenges, finding one's way despite isolation, and adaptation, can be read as an allegory with multiple interpretations. One can recall Jonathan Goldberg's observation that the parallel tracks of music and drama in melodrama can signal the existence of multiple coexisting worlds, while also illustrating a situation in which the characters may be confronted with impossible choices. The song and its performance provide an inspirational model for young people, for anyone interested in progressive social change, and for those facing adversity, like LGBTQ+ people. Lutz is also an inspiration to Tanja and Philipp as teachers, who marvel at their student's confidence. Lutz's development and his artistic advocacy of emotional clarity come at a productive moment, as Philipp departs from Tanja on the subway and is unknowingly about to meet his new love interest, Matthias, again.

A New Beginning

In one world, Philipp seems to be on a path of happiness and fulfillment. He has experienced the romantic coupling with Tanja. He has tried to make his mother proud, providing her with evidence of his relationship with Tanja; his mother seemed unconvinced, however, perhaps surmising that Philipp is gay. Although he has encountered the shock of Jakob's reappearance and the resurgence of his past, leading to his drunken visit to the gay bar, Philipp seems to have recovered and stabilized his life again. In the scene after Lutz's performance in the youth club, Philipp and Tanja sit together in a subway car. The couple lean against each other, holding hands, as both gaze out the subway window in a moment of apparent bliss. Philipp exits the subway and presses his palm up against the window; Tanja matches his with hers on the opposite side. Through the subway car window, one can see the sign for the subway stop (Marx-Engels-Platz), recalling a similar shot earlier in the film when the skinhead assailants fled the subway.

Philipp walks across Gendarmenmarkt square on his way to queue for tickets for a concert for Tanja's birthday. He walks past the French Church, and an enormous line of people comes into view as the camera captures the Concert Hall (Konzerthaus Berlin, formerly Schauspielhaus Berlin), a classical-music venue. The hall had recently been completely restored (finished in 1984) and had been the location for the opening concert of Berlin's 750th anniversary celebrations in 1987. Philipp joins the line and asks an older man in front him, who is reading a book with a pocket flashlight, how long people have been waiting. "Since yesterday morning. I'm also pretty late this time," he says, which means Philipp is even later. We next see a shot of Matthias, standing with his bicycle, apparently looking at Philipp, before we see Philipp looking past the camera. The editing of the next shots implies that Matthias and Philipp see each other, although Philipp shows no recognition of Matthias. This is not unexpected, after all, since Philipp was extremely drunk when Matthias and Walter ferried him home. After smiling slightly, Matthias climbs on his bicycle and pedals past the queue.

Coming Out's treatment of the queue in this sequence is remarkable for at least two reasons. First, it was unusual for a queue to be filmed or shown in media, let alone staged as a part of storytelling. For ideological reasons, there was a strong aversion to documenting examples of citizens faced with scarcity. As had happened after previous crises like the end of the First World War and the periods of hyperinflation (early 1920s) in the Weimar Republic, the years following the end of the Second World War had seen a recurrence of the lines for goods and necessities. This does not mean that there were never depictions of lines of people in GDR or other Eastern Bloc countries' media. Such images were sometimes deployed to serve the purposes of the regime; for example, to demonstrate the success of the state and the populace's support for its actions. It could also illustrate the popularity and acclaim of cultural offerings, as media references to sold-out concerts showed the worthiness of performing ensembles and the cultural sophistication of the population. East Germans developed vocabulary to refer to the waiting conditions they faced. One example is the "waiting community" (*Wartegemeinschaft*), a sarcastic term used to describe the queues in front of shops or state offices, playing on the frequently used "socialist community" (*sozialistische Gemeinschaft*), which was a mainstay of "real-existing socialism."[74]

The second reason the queue scene is intriguing is that it does something temporally and diegetically unexpected for the otherwise realistic mode of the film. After Matthias bicycles away, another tracking shot proceeds past some people standing in the queue. The nondiegetic music score, which strongly resembles earlier passages of music with flute and strings, starts again once Matthias and Philipp are shown and the camera passes the queue. The people are having a good time. Many laugh and smile, share food and drink, or are engaged in conversations. A descending crane shot shows a group of five sitting in a circle sharing food. We can see that not all in the queue are standing in an orderly row, with small groups of people chatting. The camera cuts to a young woman who pulls a violin out of its case and begins to play (fig. 22), adding a prominent violin line to the playing soundtrack. The music that we continue to hear, however, is also the nondiegetic score, as if the diegetic violinist magically became a part of the film score; it seems like the violin we hear in the soundtrack is what the queuing violinist is playing. In the same scene, people begin dancing, and cutaway shots show a couple

Figure 22. The violinist's music links the audience's world with that of the characters on-screen.

kissing and other people sleeping under bedcovers on foldout chairs. A long shot shows more of the people milling about on the square, before cutting to a medium shot of Matthias, who brings the film back to earth by talking to Philipp.

Combined with the editing, the nondiegetic music alters the realism of this sequence on the square and momentarily changes the film's use of time. The sequence becomes a montage for the passage of time, as the people it depicts are gathered for the purpose of waiting, a collective marking of the desire for time to pass to reach their goal: obtaining concert tickets. The mise-en-scène and cinematography, most notably the use of the crane shot, divert attention away from the film's main characters and toward the larger gathering of people, thus also altering the film's use of space. Because the music of the film's internal world in front of the camera and the soundtrack added to the film after its production coincide, this scene has the effect of involving the viewers in the scene itself. The sounds and music that the characters hear seem to be the same as what the audience hears. This resembles what Richard Dyer has called a "fantasy collectivity" in which the narrative involves the audience in an imaginary sense of joint experience or activity.[75] Although there are other sequences in *Coming Out* featuring either diegetic or nondiegetic music, the queue is one of only three sequences in the film in which there is an overlap or a transition between the two.

What we see here is different from Jean-Paul Sartre's conception of queuing in *Critique of Dialectical Reason*, that the individuals in a queue stand in "a plurality of isolations," since they do not come together for a common (higher) purpose, nor do they even usually speak to each other.[76] Sartre assumes that people waiting in line share only the goal of competing with each other for the same limited resource, in his example a bus ticket.[77] In the ticket queue in *Coming Out*, what the various shots show is precisely a sense of community, with shared food and drink, laughter and affection, dancing and interaction. The music in this sequence, too, pulls the audience into the sense of community that the people on-screen are experiencing.

While Sartre thinks about a "grouping" of individual, separate people, other scholars have also considered the temporal aspects of queuing and what it means to be waiting, especially in line. Focusing initially on experiences in Communist Romania, Katherine Verdery argues that time is "flattened" in queues, which she sees as placing individuals and their bodies in idle time.[78] Such "immobilization of bodies" diverts the individuals' energies from activities of their choosing and from actions that may be more productive or useful, like dissidence, organizing against the state, or even apolitical leisure pursuits.[79] Anna Fishzon connects the notion of queer time, developed in part by scholars like Jack Halberstam, to queues' facilitation of an experience that is somehow outside the regular passage of time and the occupation of space.[80] Like these ideas of queues' ability to draw bodies into a different use of time and space, the film's use of the camera, editing, and the music make these moments special for their appeal to and involvement of the audience. The shots of hopeful ticket-buyers develop the audience's perception of the physical space, while the music moves the audience into the space and time of what is on-screen. We join the waiting crowd and are part of the important moment in which Matthias and Philipp's romance is kindled.

The queue in *Coming Out*, corresponding to the extraordinary use of time, provides a moment for both communal engagement—what we see of the crowd and their joyful interactions—and the reconnection of Philipp and Matthias. The editing of this sequence makes it unclear how much time has passed since Matthias originally saw Philipp, about a minute and a half prior to this in screen time. We can still hear the violin music, and the film cuts to a medium shot of Matthias, who says to Philipp: "We see each other again here. Funny." This confounds Philipp, who does not recognize Matthias and thinks that Matthias is mistaking him for someone else. "Your name is Philipp!" Matthias says.

Briefly leaving the actual space of the queue, we cut to a descending crane shot that alights upon Philipp and Matthias standing close together under a tree in a medium close-up (figs. 23 and 24). They have moved off to the side of the square. The multiple crane shots in the queuing sequence are the only occurrences of this technique, further marking the use of time and space as something exceptional. The camera movements here, with the inclusion of multiple tracking and crane shots, differ from those in the rest of the film, marking a significant moment in the story and in the aesthetic approach to the unfolding of the narrative. There has been an elision here, because it has become clear to Philipp that Matthias had helped him home from the bar. Philipp shyly says he doesn't remember much from that night when Matthias first saw him. The camera abruptly returns to the world of the queue with a wide shot of the crowd and disrupts the moment that Philipp and Matthias had been sharing. A voice from the loudspeaker announces that the ticket office is now open. We see the crowd of people on the square quickly reform an orderly single line, retaking their positions in the queue (fig. 25). Again, the

Figures 23 and 24. The crane shot descends on the pair's conversation moving in position from fig. 23 to fig. 24.

camera joins Philipp in line, as he hears from the older man ahead of him about past conferences he has attended. This brief scene is an odd inclusion, but it can be read as another instance of the marking of time; in this case, Philipp and the audience are not interested in what the man has to say.

Figure 25. The camera's and audience's attention return to the task of queuing for tickets when a loudspeaker asks everyone to reassemble.

The overcoming of the queue by Philipp and Matthias and their exit is another signal that the film is reentering the other temporal world and that the time frame of the queue, with all its communal joy and the private possibility that is shown between Philipp and Matthias, is rejoining the regular order of time and space. Once Philipp and Matthias acquire their tickets, a shot tracks them as they walk past those who are still waiting. Now, Philipp disappoints Matthias, who thinks their adventure can continue. Although he says he must go, Philipp asks, "What did you think of me? I was so drunk," referring to when Matthias and Walter brought him home from the bar. Matthias's reply reveals more about the coming-out experience: "I thought of myself. It's like that when you figure out what you are. Then you go to bars and drink just to drown all your problems." He invites Philipp to his birthday party happening that night, to which Philipp seems to respond favorably and then, after a second of contemplation, realizes it won't work. "You'll make it," Matthias says, before kissing Philipp on the cheek and leaving. The expression on Philipp's face in close-up as he watches Matthias leave conveys

Figure 26. After their queuing experience, Philipp is drawn to Matthias and the possibilities he represents.

both hope and disappointment (fig. 26). Philipp's acquaintance with Matthias unveils a fantastic world of possibilities to explore his own identity and the experiences that had been foreclosed since his youthful relationship with Jakob. It also, however, exposes a glaring contradiction with the life Philipp has managed to create, even if the latter is largely a facade.

Coming Out again highlights contrast, as the editing does the queerly melodramatic work of effecting the unusual love triangle: we cut from Philipp's meaningful expression to a tranquil domestic scene. Philipp and Tanja drink mulled wine and then to go to bed, and Philipp reads aloud from *And When You'll Be the King, and When You'll Be the Executioner*, a 1968 novel by Polish author Tadeusz Nowak (1930–91). "I clicked my heels together sharply. It brought tears to my eyes. Then I realized that I was naked. I hid my manhood with my hands. I saw his mouth twitch with amusement. My nakedness disappeared in the captain's eyes." He continues reading, although he notices that Tanja has fallen asleep. "You should be ashamed of yourself, Corporal. You're shit-scared, a disgrace to the army."

Nowak's novel focuses on a troubled hero, a young man who grapples with issues of masculinity, duty, and conscience, linking Philipp with the protagonist's struggle with self-understanding and -acceptance.

Before leaving Tanja's apartment, Philipp considers Tanja and then turns off the lights and leaves the bedroom. He leaves a note for Tanja on the kitchen table: "Please don't be sad. I need to be alone for a while. Don't worry or try to contact me." Philipp is struggling with his life and who he is, and this is not purely an internal issue. He faces social consequences that extend beyond his own acceptance of his sexuality and his relationships, whether with Tanja or with a man like Matthias. This moment in which Philipp makes an initial break with Tanja marks a caesura. Part of his being alone must involve his choice of exploring the possibilities that lie ahead down another relationship path.

After a brief scene at Matthias's party, the film cuts to Philipp's apartment, where he and Matthias have arrived. Both go to the large windows with a bird's-eye view of part of the city from the high-rise building. Matthias points out a streetcar, which from this height looks like a toy. The two have ascended to another removed world, albeit temporarily. They hold hands and exchange some affectionate words. "I believe I've always been waiting for you. At least for the past two years," Matthias says. Matthias sits on Philipp's bed, and Philipp seems overcome once more with uncertainty. He wrings his hands and tells Matthias it may not have been a good idea for him to have come here. "Do you not want to have a family? Children?" Philipp asks Matthias. "No," Matthias replies. "I don't want any of that. I know I can't have it anyway."

The official emphasis on reproduction and the cishet family was one of the main reasons for the taboo on homosexuality in East Germany. Family policy and public representations of gender were exclusively heteronormative in nature, removing any possible doubt about where a citizen's priorities must lie.[81] Official state support for heteronormative, procreative families headed by a married couple began already in the early 1950s. Although the forms of this public preference changed, the underlying message remained consistent for decades. Spending time with one's family was also one of the most acceptable types of leisure.[82] The organization of GDR society, its emphasis on familial connections, and the conventional "niches" of community often led to feelings of isolation among LGBTQ+ people.[83] Philipp's concerns stem from the normative understanding that queer people could not participate in any of the structures that were valued by most of society. Matthias's response gestures toward more diverse ways of thinking about the question.

Matthias breaks the ice by telling Philipp about the erotic poems that his grandmother wrote. Their laughter at these poems leads to their undressing followed by kissing, embracing, and (between cuts) a sexual encounter, which is not directly shown, but the viewer is meant to infer it took place. As the two lie naked on Philipp's bed, Matthias speaks to the dual objective of the film, acknowledging the experience of queer viewers while also enlightening nonqueer viewers. Resting his head on Philipp's chest, Matthias says, "Do you know the feeling when you're going to bed? The feeling that someone might ring your doorbell, but no one comes. I'm talking nonsense. But yesterday, there in the cold, I noticed for the first time that I had found someone. Someone's hand to hold to make me warm inside. Then you're not alone. Maybe. Maybe it's possible." He and Philipp embrace again before the camera pans along their naked, intertwined bodies (fig. 27) and stops on a close-up of their sleeping faces directed toward each other. As the script directs, "They lie on the bed, intertwined in one another, so that one cannot tell their bodies apart. . . . Their feet, legs, thighs intertwined. Their backs, their arms. Their faces, as they sleep."[84] A brief external shot of nighttime Berlin, with its lights, traffic, and loud noises, once more reminds the viewer that the story is taking place in a larger context.

For several reasons, this sequence marks one of the high points of the film, if not exactly a climax. Close to the midpoint of the

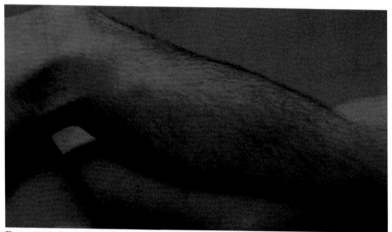

Figure 27. A first in GDR film, the portrayal of queer sexual intimacy shows the two men's bodies intertwined.

film, it signals a momentous change, especially for Philipp but also for Matthias. Although it may seem as simple as the two of them arriving at Philipp's flat, on a more symbolic level the two have entered an extraordinary time and space where they have a warm, intimate encounter. While they stand in front of the apartment's large windows, the lights of the city form a colorful backdrop, highlighting their position as two among many. Common themes in queer-oriented literature and art include the ideas that queer people are either singular individuals and alone or, perhaps more optimistically, that of the many people around them there must be more like them. The dialogue between Philipp and Matthias reveals insecurities on both their parts, but about different things. Philipp remains uncertain about what may face him if he acknowledges and embraces his true self. Matthias is confident in his own identity and knows more about who he is, although he is also seeking companionship. The characters' interaction reveals much about the experiences of many queer people, not just in East Germany. As David Brandon Dennis has argued, "This is the first real love scene in the film; those between Philipp and Tanja show little or no actual intimacy."[85] As the first such depiction of characters engaged in any kind of homosexual interaction in a GDR feature film, it remains remarkable that it was made at all. Philipp and Matthias gradually increase their intimacy, moving from talking to light physical touch to, eventually, the sexual encounter that is strongly implied if not shown. Each stage of this homosexual intimacy is more radical than the previous one, progressing toward the final panning shot of their postcoital tranquility.

In Philipp's apartment the morning after, a mostly quiet comfort still reigns. Car horns and yelling children from the street below occasionally disrupt the silence. Matthias, now dressed, sits on the bed and says to Philipp, "I think you're incredible." Philipp admits with a small smile, "I was never with a guy before." The open-ended yet warm and positive nature of Philipp's parting from Matthias could make one believe that Philipp has found a new path. This comes, after all, after he has left the note for Tanja. The contrasting melodramatic structure of the narrative, however, now pulls Philipp in a different direction.

Coming Out and Reconciling Identities

Whereas the previous part of the film had shown Philipp's exploration of his identity, another part of his coming out now occurs, as parts of his life collide. The film now brings the viewer back to the other part of Philipp's life. This is the parallel track on which his job as a teacher strongly relates to his public, heterosexual, normative persona, where he is also possibly still in a relationship with Tanja. A shot of the school's courtyard shows Philipp and Frau Möllemann talking while they supervise the students on a break between classes. After telling Philipp that he looks like he's coming down with something, Frau Möllemann surprises him with a new possibility: "Tanja is showing it more. One could think that she's pregnant."

"What?!" Philipp replies. "'One *could think*,' I said. That's all," she says. "You wouldn't be overjoyed, I guess." Tanja hasn't said anything, but "When a woman gets dizzy spells and always has to throw up. . . ." Philipp rushes back into the school building. A transition shot shows Philipp and Tanja walking toward Tanja's apartment. The camera pans to follow them crossing the street and rounding a corner. One can see that they have been talking, although Tanja reacts very little, but the only sounds present are the loud noises of the city and traffic. According to the script, Philipp is encouraging Tanja to go to a doctor.

> Tanja: Oh, please!
> Philipp: You should. Or were you . . . did you already . . . ?
> Tanja: Why would I?
> Tanja looks uncomprehendingly at Philipp.
> Philipp: You can't . . . you just can't trifle with that.
> Tanja (annoyed): With what? I take some medicine at
>   home and that's it.[86]

They are talking about Tanja having an abortion. It is unclear whether this would explain why the filmmakers removed the conversation's audio. It is also possible that the sound quality was merely insufficient for inclusion in the film. Many other scenes had to be rerecorded in postproduction, because the cameras used for the film were so noisy.

Like other topics related to gender and sexuality, abortion has a complicated history in Germany, which can be mentioned here only briefly. In 1950 the GDR recriminalized abortion except in cases where the mother's health was threatened; but in 1972 it legalized all abortions in the first trimester. Legalization of abortion, however, did not mean that GDR governmental policy encouraged women to avail themselves of this possibility. On the contrary, GDR society was intensely dedicated to the proposition of fostering procreative heterosexual marriage and the families that resulted from it. GDR policies encouraged larger families in the 1970s; these efforts continued in the face of declining birth rates in the 1980s. The state had to walk a fine line between recognizing women's legal rights to abortions and fostering more births, which would support the economy and the national project.[87] Abortion law and policies went on to become one of the most hotly debated issues surrounding German unification in 1990 and the harmonization of the two Germanys' legal systems.[88] In West Germany, abortion was regulated as a crime but deemed "not punishable" under certain limited circumstances.[89] As the West German situation took precedence starting in 1990, GDR women faced new restrictions on access to abortions in unified Germany.

In Tanja's apartment, the couple continues the conversation. It is another version of a domestic scene, as Philipp and Tanja do the dishes and one can see a charming wreath of flowers on the kitchen door, but they are having an argument about the pregnancy. Storming into the next room to clean more dishes off the table, Tanja tells Philipp he has to decide whether to stay or leave. Philipp replies, "I won't abandon you. Never." Searching for more information about what had occupied Philipp during his time away from her, Tanja says, "Maybe it's my fault that you suddenly wanted a new girl-friend." Philipp then confirms Tanja's suspicion, in a way: "I want to stay with you. I don't want it to happen again—" Philipp cuts himself off when he realizes what he has acknowledged, although he has not revealed that he became involved with a man. The argument ends with Tanja telling Philipp in exasperation that she loves him, breaking a plate on the floor, and leaving the room. Philipp's decision not to leave Tanja and their child leads to the uneasy air of reconciliation one sees between them in the following sequence.

In another of the film's contrasts, the viewer sees Matthias searching for Philipp at the latter's apartment. Matthias has a bouquet of flowers in his hand and rings at Philipp's door, but there is no answer. Philipp's door has several notes affixed to it. The shot recalls both the earlier scene after Matthias and Walter brought Philipp home from the bar and, with the flowers, the prior scene, mimicking the wreath of flowers on Tanja's kitchen door. One can barely make out that one note says, "Where are you? I'm waiting. Matthias." As Matthias leaves, nondiegetic music begins to play and transitions to the following sequence: Johann Sebastian Bach's *Christmas Oratorio* (BWV 248). An establishing shot taken from some distance shows a Christmas market at night with its festive lights situated amid the bustle of the city. Still holding the bouquet, Matthias walks through the crowded market toward a ring-toss booth. The camera pans to a woman working at the booth, bundled up in winter attire including a large ushanka and holding the rings on her arm. A close-up of Matthias's face captures him considering the woman, and there is a minuscule movement on his face, the smallest barely recognizable move toward a smile, before he dejectedly hands the bouquet to the woman at the booth. She smiles sheepishly, admiring the flowers. Just as Matthias gives away the bouquet, the choir ironically declares, "Cheer, rejoice! Praise these days!" Shots follow of Matthias walking away from the booth and through the market. His isolation is clear as he maneuvers past happy families, many playing games and enjoying the festive atmosphere.

Like in previous sequences (Philipp's move to Tanja's accompanied by Mozart's *Magic Flute* or the violinist's performance for the concert ticket queue), here nondiegetic music becomes diegetic or these categories blend into each other. The *Christmas Oratorio* starts as musical accompaniment for Matthias's walk through the Christmas market. The choice of this oratorio, and specifically this choral number, is simultaneously an incongruous addition (because of its triumphant tone juxtaposed with Matthias's despondence) and wholly appropriate (because of the Christmas season). Then the source of the music and the film's story meet. We cut to the Concert Hall, in front of which Philipp had been waiting in the ticket queue: Tanja hoped for the tickets as a birthday gift. A long shot of the venue's stage shows the members of the choir and orchestra performing Bach's work for a full audience, as the music grandly transitions with trumpets, timpani, and strings.[90] The camera cuts to a medium shot of Philipp and Tanja in the audience. Tanja intently gazes forward, watching the performance with rapt attention; Philipp turns to her and touches her hand (fig. 28). They have at least temporarily reconciled since their earlier argument. This tender moment between them is the most important part of the sequence, as it provides background for the dramatic meeting soon to take place during intermission in the Concert Hall's lobby.

Given the time of year in which *Coming Out*'s story takes place, the selection of the *Christmas Oratorio* to figure in the film's music, both its use as nondiegetic soundtrack and as diegetic concert performance, is not surprising. The rousing and imposing opening chorus, which is the only portion of the work included in *Coming Out*, sets the tone for most of the oratorio. Beyond the praise that the first movement exhibits, though, there is a persistent theme of love, often communicated through the common Christian imagery

Figure 28. Tanja and Philipp attend the Bach concert, and there are signs their relationship may have improved.

of the bridegroom and bride, earthly relationships that have been made spiritual.[91] In *Coming Out*, Matthias's isolation has been simultaneously linked to the reunification of Philipp and Tanja, whose reconciliation, likely parenthood, and marital union—in the following sequence Philipp first calls Tanja "my wife"—are symbolically bolstered by the music.

Whatever temporary bliss or truce may be implied by Philipp and Tanja's attendance at the concert and Philipp's conciliatory look is short-lived. At intermission, the audience mills about in the lobby with drinks. Tanja gets in line for champagne and drops something, which Matthias, who has wandered into the lobby looking for Philipp, picks up and gives back to her. The audience can predict what is about to happen. Tanja sees Philipp and Matthias find each other and exuberantly embrace. Tanja approaches and sees them continuing to hug and affectionately touch each other, finally saying, "Here's the champagne." Neither Philipp nor Matthias notices her. As Matthias continues to stroke Philipp's hair and tell him about his efforts to find him, a tracking medium close-up of Tanja rotates slightly, showing both her isolation and her fixation on the two men in front of her, before she eventually moves in closer and repeats her offer of the champagne. Philipp finally must acknowledge her presence (fig. 29). Dagmar Manzel, as Tanja, artfully delivers the deep, confused awkwardness of this moment, with the help of skilled camerawork by cinematographer Martin Schlesinger.

The awkward quickly becomes tragic. Philipp manages to introduce Matthias to Tanja and then reveals the background to the conciliation we had seen before: "This is Tanja. My wife. Yes, this is Tanja. My wife." Dirk Kummer as Matthias beautifully conveys a quiet dejection, as his character absorbs the shock of Philipp's new information and is crushed. A single tear falls down his cheek as his hopes collapse. That Philipp and Tanja are married is also news to the viewer, because there was no previous mention of this. Matthias's first quiet "I see" then becomes a second, quieter and more resigned

Figure 29. Matthias's delight at seeing Philipp soon changes to despair when he learns of Philipp and Tanja's reconciliation.

"I see." He repeats it a third time, even more quietly, as he leaves and looks back at Philipp, who runs after him out of the Concert Hall and onto the square in front of the building (the site of the earlier ticket queue and the pair's first interactions). Once again, Tanja is left alone, and a shot captures her standing by herself in the crowded lobby, holding the two glasses of champagne (fig. 30).

This intermission scene puts on display some of the most crucial relationship dynamics at work in *Coming Out*. Here, we find a staging of the love triangle described earlier as well as an iteration of broader realities of socialist society. The shots following the dramatic camera rotation on Tanja capture the triangular relationship's constituents inhabiting the same space (fig. 29). Philipp must uncomfortably manage the relationship lines he has with Matthias and Tanja, in a queered version of the conventional romantic competition. A customary heterosexual love triangle would feature a rivalry between the two men in the trio, who ostensibly desire the woman. This moment of their interaction (fig. 29) illustrates the characters' lines of desire: Matthias gazes at Philipp; Tanja looks expectantly at

Figure 30. Philipp chases after Matthias and leaves Tanja alone and confused in the crowd of concertgoers.

Philipp; and Philipp looks to the floor, unable to choose between his two entanglements. Finally, once Philipp runs after Matthias, Tanja's solitary stance with the glasses of champagne shows her as the obstacle in a line between the two men.

The shot of Tanja standing alone cuts to a medium shot of Philipp in a café, sitting across from Tanja right after they have left the concert. The truth has come out: "I wasn't hiding it from you. Not on purpose," Philipp says. On top of feeling frustrated and betrayed, Tanja feels stupid for not having noticed anything or figured it all out. "I want to explain everything to you," Philipp says. Tanja has had enough and says that her birthday wish is for Philipp to disappear. With this she storms out of the café. Tanja's isolation shows her sympathetically as one of the victims of Philipp's belated acknowledgment of his sexuality. *Coming Out*'s depiction of Tanja demonstrates that it is not just Philipp and Matthias who are negatively affected by social conventions and Philipp's need to hide. The stigma associated with being gay, based on moralistic social conventions, ends up hurting many people.

While his personal life falls apart, Philipp's professional life is not immune to disturbance either. Philipp arrives late to school and is reprimanded by the principal. In class, Philipp erupts with frustration when a pair of students misbehave, whispering and snickering as Lutz recites a poem by Johann Wolfgang von Goethe. Poetry recitation is a change from Philipp's teaching methods one saw earlier in the film, when he danced with his students, everyone was engaged, and the activity was interrupted by the principal's unexpected entry into the classroom. The poem Lutz recites, known as "Mignon" after the character who delivers it, is one of the most famous in German literature. Mignon and her song's verses appear in Goethe's *Wilhelm Meister's Apprenticeship* (1795–96) (and an earlier fragment, *Wilhelm Meister's Theatrical Calling*). Mignon is an unusual, androgynous, and enigmatic character whose presentation in the novel has inspired many interpretations, including some concentrating on her gendered and sexual qualities. The poem is mysterious in that it alludes to an impressive, welcoming place of natural beauty and classically constructed grandeur, while also invoking varied motifs of danger, a need for protection, dragons, and familial bonds. Its placement here gives Mignon's secretive voice to Lutz, a character who, the viewer will later find out, is also gay.

Philipp's agitation leads him to search for Matthias in subsequent scenes. We see Philipp at the gay bar where he first encountered Matthias (or, more accurately, where Matthias first saw Philipp). As Philipp begins to leave the bar, he says to the waiter, Achim, "Someone must know his name and where he lives." Achim pauses before replying, "Nobody knows anybody's name or address here. Here, everyone is alone. And everyone is afraid." With this slightly melodramatic gesture, the film aims to communicate the isolation felt by many in queer communities, whether in East Berlin or elsewhere. Despite the decriminalization of homosexuality in 1968, LGBTQ+ people's lives had not changed overnight; nor had their existence suddenly ceased to be a taboo or a socially undesirable reality. Beyond the widespread isolation, exacerbated by difficulty in meeting like-minded people, especially for those outside of large cities, there remained a fear among many that they could be the target of government surveillance, other homophobic actions, or at least the judgment and ridicule of those around them, including their families.

Philipp is left alone, trying to reconcile his feelings and to come to terms with both himself and his new position in the world. His relationships have crumbled, and the stability he once had in his life, built up behind a false facade, has deteriorated. Alone in his apartment in the next scene, Philipp smokes and is restless while he listens to a song by Silly, "Snow-White Day," sung by Tamara Danz. The song, which touches on themes of understanding oneself and one's surroundings and recognizing when appearances can be false, includes a line in its refrain: "I feel hollow in my own skin." He starts to masturbate while standing in front of a mirror. His pained facial expressions illustrate his inability to think about other things, to distract himself, and his occasional glances at the mirror punctuate these moments with unaccepting discomfort (fig. 31).

Acceptance

Another turning point for Philipp arrives when his mother shows up unexpectedly at the school where he works, seeking him out after his recent incommunicability. Walking in a park, Philipp breaks the news to her about his homosexuality. She has asked him several questions, including why it must be that he is "this way." She walks toward the camera and just to the right as he frustratedly says, "That's the way it is," and responds to her questions: "And why must it be that I have to justify myself? Why? Is it better to pretend, lie to oneself? To try to force something that one can't force? To make others unhappy, because there is no other alternative? Because nature made me this way? Who am I harming? Besides my so-called good

Figure 31. Philipp's agitated contemplation of his reflection shows his continued wrestling with his sexual identity.

Figure 32. Talking to his mother, who is off-camera, Philipp delivers a forceful defense of individuals' self-determination.

reputation? Doesn't everyone have the right to live how they must?" Philipp demonstrates his breakthrough in this vindication of queer people, which is delivered almost as though he speaks directly to the audience (fig. 32). His mother is overcome with sadness, begins crying, and runs away after expressing her disappointment. It is the first time in the film he has been explicit about his sexuality, revealing that he has come to a place of acceptance in a way that he never had before. Philipp's conversation with his mother also marks the first deliberate enactment of the film's title, although his coming out has been in process for some time.

Following Philipp's acknowledgment of his identity, the remaining time of the film, approximately twenty minutes, concentrates primarily on two narrative strands. The first is Philipp's ongoing search for Matthias, with his hope of potentially reconciling with him. The second is Philipp's struggle to fully accept himself and to understand the direction of his life and position within society. In the former strand, Philipp repeatedly visits locations in the gay scene in his efforts to find Matthias. In the latter strand, Philipp explores connections to other gay men, both intentionally (through cruising) and coincidentally in a later conversation with Walter, the older man who had helped him get home. Both strands serve the purposes of narrative development and resolution while also adding to the film's unprecedented depiction of aspects of queer life.

In two sequences, Philipp searches for Matthias in different gay bars. In the first sequence, which lasts less than a minute, Philipp enters a bar and looks around intensely for Matthias. In a different bar, Philipp sees Matthias and then approaches and awkwardly embraces him, stroking his hair. Matthias pulls away, reproaches Philipp about his wife, and pulls his date (Philipp's student, Lutz) onto the dance floor and sadly embraces him. That Lutz is there is a surprise to the viewer and to Philipp. Lutz comforts Matthias, but repeatedly looks over at Philipp, who soon leaves the bar.

Between these two sequences that show Philipp's search for Matthias, the film reveals another facet of gay life: cruising. The film situates the cruising in Volkspark Friedrichshain, one of the larger parks in Berlin. Some of the action takes place around the Fairy Tale Fountain, where the viewer sees several men loitering or pacing; the area is surprisingly crowded. In other shots, one sees men in the woods, variously alone or in couples, sometimes waiting and other times kissing, sometimes in silhouette and others in moonlight. More shots show men entering and exiting the public toilets. While the scene is furtive, there is a great deal of motion, mostly pacing up and down—movement without an actual destination. Philipp moves around, too, and eventually pairs up with a young man (René Schmidt) who comes back to Philipp's apartment. There is little verbal communication between them, and the little there is occurs only after they have had sex.

Coming Out's depiction of cruising and its role in sexual and romantic relationships walks a line between disapproving and pitying. According to the film's script, "A curious oppressive silence pervades the scene. Always the same path—this way then that way—the path of these silent men."[92] It is "a secret magnetism" that keeps Philipp there, apparently making it unlikely that Philipp or others could *choose* to be there.[93] The scene in the script is sordid: one of men passing hand signals to each other, of older men taking advantage of younger men (possibly paying for sex). The filmmakers got some aspects right, like location, but the crowd of men shown in the film is conspicuously large. Instead of allowing Philipp to find a supplement or even a desirable replacement for what he had with Tanja or Matthias, the film posits that cruising and casual, anonymous sex is merely a pit stop on the way toward other self-realization and intimacy, conventionally to be found in a monogamous relationship. Scholars like Sarah Ensor have argued, however, that cruising can be a space where "impersonality" can lead to intimacy rather than suppressing it.[94] Philipp must reach another low level of despair, however, before he can rise to the acceptance that the film aims to show in its conclusion.

After his rejection by Matthias, Philipp arrives at the other gay bar where he had his first real foray into the gay scene. Now, Philipp's entire world has changed. Throughout most of this sequence in the bar, Philipp behaves oddly, already slightly drunk. As he makes his way through the bar, Philipp holds a small bouquet of droopy flowers (recalling Matthias's bouquet), handing them out to men he passes. The handheld camera tracks Philipp's wandering through the bar, and the viewer is able to follow his sight line as he looks at pairs of men kissing or showing affection to one another. His strange behavior escalates as he tries to join a pair of men sitting at the bar, resting his arms on their shoulders, tries to take a drink from another group sitting at a table, and takes a cigarette from someone else at the bar. His misbehavior reaches a climax when he enters a side room where a drag queen is performing the famous standard "Can Love Be a Sin?" ("Kann denn Liebe Sünde sein?"). Philipp stands directly in front of the performer and begins loudly sing-shouting a birthday song. Most of the audience stares at Philipp, as the performer stops singing, but Walter, the older man who had helped Matthias bring Philipp home earlier in the film, approaches Philipp and tries to pull him away from the stage. Philipp stops singing and shouts, "Don't touch me, you horny old man!" They struggle and both fall. Philipp quickly stands back up and is suddenly detained by the waiter, Achim. Walter calms the situation and orders drinks. Walter and Philipp sit at a nearby table, and one of Philipp's final learning experiences, perhaps the most crucial, of the film begins. When Achim leaves the room to fetch the drinks, the camera catches the young femme white man who was assaulted in the subway-station hallway earlier in the film when Philipp ran away. Now these two men's lives are reconnected, and Philipp is in the more vulnerable position, while the younger man self-assuredly orders a drink.

The song that Philipp interrupted, "Can Love Be a Sin?," has a long history that relates to the story that Walter tells Philipp. The film's use of it in this moment is another instance of the filmmakers' propensity for adding layers of intertextual meaning, often through music. Bruno Balz (1902–88), the lyricist who had written the songs and some of the dialogue for the popular 1933 film musical *Viktor und Viktoria* (*Victor and Victoria*, directed by Reinhold Schünzel), wrote the song's text in 1938; composer Lothar Brühne (1900–1958) wrote the music. The song appeared in the unsuccessful film *The Blue Fox* (1938), a comedy starring Zarah Leander (1907–81). Like Marlene Dietrich before her, whom she succeeded as a film star, Leander became an icon for queer and trans people.[95] Also as with Dietrich, there is a long tradition of Leander impersonators. The stars' appearances, personalities, and deeper voices, giving an air of gender ambiguity, made them appealing to queer audiences. Unlike the film in which it appeared, "Can Love Be a Sin?" became popular, with its advocacy of love for love's sake. Balz's songs, like "Can Love Be a Sin?" and "The World Won't Go Under" ("Davon geht die Welt nicht unter"), which was a hit during the Nazi years, often had hidden subtexts. Balz's trademark hidden messages in his lyrics also made this song an anthem for queer audiences, for whom certain other songs and cultural touchstones served as shibboleths. For an artist like Balz, who had experienced persecution because of his homosexuality, these songs were a way to communicate with multiple audiences simultaneously: those who only heard the lyrics and the vulnerable group, to which he belonged, who could comprehend the lyrics' connotation.

The lyricist Balz had personal history relating to the film's subject and Walter's story. Balz was arrested under the antihomosexuality law (§175) in 1936 and 1941. For the latter infraction, some sources say he was arrested and sent to solitary confinement with the Gestapo, while others say he was sent to a concentration camp. Either way, he was released when a replacement lyricist could not be found to write songs for another Leander film, *The Great Love* (1942).[96]

Walter's history, which is similar to that of Bruno Balz, helps put him in a position to offer Philipp sage advance. "You think we always make a pass at every man we approach? Just because we're gay?" Walter asks. "Perhaps we're just wanting to help, like other people." In alternating shots, a drag performer dressed in a white blouse and gingham skirt and sporting a wig with horizontally extended pigtails dances and lip-synchs Chris Doerk's spirited song "Kariert" ("Plaid" [or "Checked"]). Bargoers are shown singing along and enjoying the performance. Meanwhile, sobbing and barely able to speak, Philipp reveals his horror at his gayness, that he is terrified at the prospect of being alone, and more so of being a gay teacher. "It could be worse," Walter responds dryly, while the drag performer kicks her legs up and down and dances behind him. As David Brandon Dennis has observed, this scene "styles the flamboyant cheerfulness of the subculture as a farcical performance."[97] The exuberant joy of the queer locale—the vibrantly colorful space one saw when Philipp first entered the bar earlier in the film—provides a respite from the eternally gray exterior of the GDR, but it cannot prevent the latter's occasional intrusion. The antiqueer past and present intermittently surface despite the efforts of everyone inside to keep them at bay.

The viewer has seen Philipp's loss of control and the difficulties he has faced. His troubles have included his destroyed relationships and his position of being under suspicion at his workplace. In stark contrast to both the dancing drag queen and Philipp's comparatively minor problems, Walter describes his life as a gay man of an earlier generation, living under the Nazis, and being imprisoned in a concentration camp. Walter's monologue illustrates a connected community as well as a grim melancholic picture of reality for the inhabitants of the world inside the bar. The diegetic music shifts from the cheerful "Kariert" to the hard rock "Dynamit" ("Dynamite") by Dieter Wiesjahn. In this moment, Walter, the oldest person in the bar, establishes his credentials as one who has suffered because of his sexuality. "I have paid my dues to be able to sit here and drink and wait. Wait like everyone here. For a man who smiles. Honest, loving, and tender. It's easy to do this nowadays." Walter tells Philipp of his great love, Karl, and how their same-sex relationship was discovered, prompting their imprisonment in solitary confinement before Walter was finally sent to a concentration camp. As Walter continues with his story, all the while downing shots of brandy, the camera cuts to various shots around the bar showing men smoking and drinking, their eyes wandering around. The didactic moment, in which Walter communicates to Philipp and the viewer the advantages and disadvantages of the GDR's approach to identity, comes when Walter finishes describing his own experience as a member of the Communist Party: "The comrades saved me. We worked to stop humans' exploitation of each other, so that now it doesn't matter if one is a Jew or whatever," he says, slightly slurring his words (fig. 33). "Except for the gays. We forgot them," Walter concludes before he rises from the table and walks out of the shot. "The gays" are not only an afterthought; they are actively omitted from the country's work of inclusion. The music stops with ringing guitars, dissolving into the sound of loud conversation in the bar, as we see Philipp sitting alone at a table, a score of empty brandy glasses littering the tabletop.

In this powerful scene, Walter has leveled one of the most successful forms of critique: one that embeds disapproval in its praise.

Figure 33. Surrounded by the bargoers' light-heartedness, Walter's somber monologue comforts Philipp and critiques East German tolerance.

It was a kind of criticism that was becoming more possible only in the final years of East Germany's existence, as discontent increased and the regime allowed slow reforms. Walter's recounting of this personal story and its relationship to the struggle for equality fits well within the kind of antifascist narrative that East Germany had long prized. He praises the egalitarian work of the socialist nation while criticizing it for its contradictory perspectives on same-sex affection and relationships. Walter's critique also posits homosexuality and antiqueer prejudice as problems that reach far beyond the individual. The scene echoes this by occasionally shifting the camera's attention to other people in the bar, illustrating that Philipp is not alone in feeling isolated. If socialist society can squarely face the continuing problems that many of its citizens face (which the film illustrates through its allusions to antiqueer prejudice, racism, youth discontent, and far-right violence), then it can fulfill its own potential while facilitating the self-acceptance of its people.

Philipp's concern about being a gay teacher was not a fabulation. In a striking moment following one of the first test screenings of the film, an event that was recorded on audiotape, a gay teacher spoke up. Beyond his own voiced admission of his nervousness, one can hear the anxiety in his voice as he addresses the filmmakers and the audience. Not being out yet, he is insecure and uneasy speaking so openly about the topic and even being at the screening. The man's main question relates to representation, specifically what he sees as the stereotypes presented in the film, especially the carnivalesque scenes in the bar.[98] The filmmakers' responses, like some of the reviews of the film, point to how the individuals and groups are shown in the film. That is, according to Carow and Witt, people were not shown in the film in a way that was (meant to be) exploitative or sensationalistic. As Kurt Starke had written in his expert testimonial supporting the film's production, the film was dealing with a complicated topic with a minefield of stereotypes.[99] Although Carow and Witt remark that they did not want to suppress the reality of gay life, they do not completely explain their thinking behind which stereotypes they might have perpetuated.

The film's final two sequences provide hints that Philipp has reached his goal of better understanding himself and his place in the world. The penultimate scene takes us back to Philipp's classroom. The school's principal makes an unexpected classroom visit, telling Philipp that "Certain events, which we must discuss at another time, unfortunately force us to institute increased classroom observations of your work, today unannounced." The principal ushers in three other teachers (including Frau Möllemann, who had commented on the school's atmosphere and on the possibility that Tanja was pregnant), and they sit at the back of the classroom. The camera captures the quiet and awkward scene: Philipp looks around and sits on a stool at the front of the room; one of the observing teachers removes her glasses and wearily rubs her eyes; concerned, Frau Möllemann watches Philipp at the front of the room. The students are uncertain about what is happening. They watch Philipp, and Lutz glances around and back toward the visiting teachers. The cameras used on the film made a great deal of noise, lending a mechanical hum as a sound accompaniment. (This is one of the film's scenes that had to be rerecorded by actors to make up for the poor audio quality.) At one point, Philipp gazes out the window; in an eye line match cut, the camera shows an outside courtyard and moves slowly toward the window. One sees more buildings with doorways and many windows. A leafless tree reaches into the area framed by the window. Sunlight brightens the facades of some of the buildings and casts a shadow marking a clear line on the ground. "Mr. Klahrmann!" the principal exclaims, put off by the extended silence and inactivity. A shot of Philipp half-sitting on the instructor's desk tracks backward as he looks back at the class, stands, walks a few steps forward, hooks his thumbs in his pockets (fig. 34), and says simply, "Yes."

The film's script had envisioned a more elaborate extended monologue for Philipp and a more obvious coming out. Over

Figure 34. Philipp's confident "Yes" points to a brighter future in which he acknowledges his identity and finds acceptance in society.

multiple pages, Philipp explicitly describes what he has come to terms with: "In the past few months and weeks I have recognized that I am homosexual. Because of it I have lived a life full of lies . . . concealment and . . . fear. Fear of everyone, my colleagues and you, my students. . . . I betrayed someone I loved and lost someone who means very, very much to me. . . . I know it's a risk to tell you all of this. But there is no other way for me. I'm gay, as they say. I can't live differently and don't want to."[100] Matthias Freihof, playing Philipp, found this monologue awkward. He managed to convince Carow and Witt to change the scene, so that Philipp vaguely answers all questions at once with his single "Yes." In this way he acknowledges the call from the principal while also answering the questions that have been hanging over his head: Is he gay? Will he accept himself for who and what he is? Will he move forward and continue as a teacher? Will he claim his place in society? Is there a place for him in this society? The principal and other teachers who sit in and observe Philipp's class, prompted by "certain events," hear Philipp's general yet categorical affirmation on behalf of the wider GDR society beyond the school's walls.

In the closing sequence, Philipp's newfound and confident opti‑
mism persists. One aspect that is emphasized in the film's script
but diminished in the final product is the importance of young
people for the GDR's future. The script makes clear how attached
the students are to Philipp—more so than the film itself, where the
students find him a novelty, a younger teacher who dresses more like
them, speaks to them differently than their other teachers, and gives
them unconventional assignments. The earlier sequence in which
Philipp criticizes the students for their unimaginative responses
to the Brecht poem—or rather, encourages them to think more
daringly—is one example of the clear-eyed but hopeful recognition
of the GDR's current faults as well as its promise. In the last shots
of the film, Philipp's own positivity communicates the possibilities
ahead of Philipp and therefore also ahead of the children and the
country. Mirroring the shots containing the main title credits after
Matthias's New Year's Eve suicide attempt and hospital stay, one
sees the same busy intersection, now on a bright, sunny day. Philipp
leaves his building and rides his bicycle out into the streets of
Berlin, joining the bustling traffic made up almost entirely of
Trabants. A cyclist amidst a sea of cars, he rides on as a hopeful
individual (fig. 35).

Coming Out does the decisive work of exploding the conventional
(heteronormative) romantic expectations for a relationship story. The
film began by playing with the idea of a love story and the triangular
relationship that might structure it. By now, nearly all has collapsed.
From the triangle, Philipp stands alone without Matthias or Tanja.
The Bruno Balz song "Can Love Be a Sin?," Walter's life and his
critique of society's development—all have helped to cement the
futility of a conventional narrative and its happy ending in a society
that will not allow it. The experiences that the film highlights—from
the skinheads' assault of the Black man and Tanja's isolation to the
outcomes of Philipp's and Matthias's relationships—demonstrate
that, especially when social expectations do not match people's

Figure 35. Mirroring the earlier shots (fig. 5), this sequence puts Philipp in the same physical location but in a much more confident mental and emotional position.

realities, the situation becomes far more complicated. In other words, a conventional happy ending for Philipp is not available, for instance, nor is it necessarily what he might wish for himself. With tolerance and more freedom, people like Philipp can determine what their own happy endings might entail. Philipp's affirmative positioning is a surprising product of the film's melodramatic techniques. Recalling Jonathan Goldberg's assertion that melodrama creates "a space of irresolution," there is not definitive narrative resolution in *Coming Out*.[101] One of the primary drivers of the film's plot and Philipp's uncertainty, the queered love triangle, has fallen apart without the triumph of either of the "competitors" for Philipp. Whatever expectations for a conventional happy ending—or one in which Philipp finds contentment in a relationship with either Tanja or Matthias—that the film may have created, including in its use of multiple genre devices like romantic comedy tropes, have been abandoned. Instead, this ending is an optimistic one, perhaps naively so, but it imagines a possible outcome for Philipp in which he confidently stands alone. Thus, the conclusion of the film means to signal, if not resolution for Philipp—he does not find a partner—then at least a positive future for him: he does break out of the unhappiness of denying his queerness; and by extension for LGBTQ+ people in East Germany.

Release, Reception, and Legacy

Hans Dieter Mäde, the penultimate general director of DEFA, gave his reluctant approval of the final cut on July 5, 1989.[102] Despite his prejudices, in his recommendation to the Ministry for Culture, which gave final approval of films, he wrote, "We hope that ... the belief with and because of which the film was made, namely in a moving and rousing manner to bring about tolerance, mutual understanding and integration, not only for homosexuals, but also for any minorities in our society, would find expression.... We would attach great importance to such an effect in light of diverse neofascist, xenophobic, violent tendencies in many parts of our contemporary world."[103] The director of DEFA's international distribution branch, Helmut Diller, acknowledged that there might be difficulties with the sale of the film. It was difficult to predict, Diller wrote, how other countries might receive the film, based on differing social and cultural understandings of homosexuality, since there were already problems with the distribution of some films even based on their display of relationships between men and women.[104] Nonetheless, the branch prepared videocassettes and information materials in various languages to prepare for widespread interest. Similarly, Progress Film, then the sole distributor of DEFA films internationally, wanted to be sure to have enough copies of the film available for wide distribution, partly to support the idea of tolerance that the film aimed to foster.[105]

As we have seen, Carow used a conventional, heteronormative form to tell an unconventional, nonheteronormative story. I have discussed above how especially Carow, Witt, and Schlesinger, but also the actors and others involved in making the film took the components of a traditional, melodramatic love story—the relationship between Philipp and Tanja—and shaped them into a queer pastiche of such a love story. How would the public react? *Coming Out*'s premiere took place in the Kino International on Karl-Marx-Allee on November 9, 1989—as it happened, the theater's last East German premiere. Stories about the film and advertisements announcing a story about "another kind of love" had piqued curiosity about the film in the months and weeks prior to its release.[106] The first screening at 7:30 p.m. had sold out far in advance, so the theater added a second showing at 10:00 p.m. On November 9, by the time the first screening had finished, news that the Wall had been breached and that the GDR's borders were now open was already spreading. From the large windows in the theater lobby, members of the cast could see increased traffic and thought that something must be happening.[107] Alongside the news they were hearing, though, the fact remained that another monumental event had taken place: a landmark film had been created and released into the world.

Coming Out's focus on urban gay life prompted many questions from LGBTQ+ people outside Berlin about its sole focus on life there. In a discussion with the audience after a test screening in September 1989, Witt answered a question about the possibilities of including places like Leipzig or Rostock by arguing it would not have been possible to film elsewhere. Berlin was the location of the most developed queer subculture, with bars and other locations that could be readily accessed, which would not have been as possible in smaller cities and definitely not in towns.[108] A common observation about the locations and people shown in the film was that they had a documentary quality, even if not in their intent. As film historian, activist, and author Vito Russo wrote in *The Advocate*, "The film provides a last look at gay locations and gay life in East Berlin before the wall came down."[109]

Already by the day of the premiere it was apparent that *Coming Out*'s themes had relevance far beyond the film's story. In a piece that ran in the newspaper aligned with the Christian Democratic Union, *Neue Zeit*, that day, an interview with Matthias Freihof had the following introduction: "With 'Coming out' Heiner Carow has made an issue of the sexual difference of many people. It's not just about homosexuality; rather, it's also about assertions of honesty and personality as well as acceptance and tolerance of those who think and feel differently. These are questions that are very serious and important to us these weeks."[110] Although the total collapse of the GDR was not yet certain, the news prior to November 9, 1989, had tracked a great deal of upheaval. Massive demonstrations aimed at democratic reforms of the GDR, which had begun weeks before, continued, including the so-called Monday Demonstrations in cities like Leipzig, Dresden, and Rostock. The day before the premiere, the news reported that the Council of Ministers, the country's highest body, had resigned.[111] In an effort to meet, in some measure, the demonstrators' demands for reform, the regime announced it would reform the procedures for allowing East Germans to travel outside of the country. Citizens were publicly criticizing the national surveillance culture instituted by the Stasi. It was clear that *Coming Out* had arrived in circumstances that could not have been predicted even a year prior.

Despite the atmosphere of social and political upheaval into which the film arrived, most of the journalistic and critical reactions to the film considered it largely on its own terms. Overall, the reaction to the film was positive; the basis for the reception varied widely. Those writing about *Coming Out* overwhelmingly complimented the filmmaking. Most such commentary was aimed at Carow's directing, but Witt's writing and Schlesinger's camerawork were also highly praised. The reviewers recognized that social difference and the tendency to persecute it are themes of the film, even when they simplify the processes at work or overstate how accepting of difference the real-life GDR was.[112] Some elements like the Communist-themed scene between Walter and Philipp found mixed reception, variously coming across as overdone or deeply moving. Helmut Ullrich wrote that the film's message can be extended to those who think differently, and that it arrived at a time when "so many taboos are disintegrating and intolerance is dwindling away."[113] The ruling party-aligned newspaper *Neues Deutschland* conceded that many people who are different have been "driven into a ghetto of their feelings, a public hiding game, a life in niches, which has often enough led to frustration and endless isolation."[114] Some reviews specifically mentioned the delicate treatment of the intimacy between Philipp and Matthias, an even more pronounced first for GDR media than just the portrayal of homosexuality in a feature film.[115] By December 1, when Monika Zimmermann wrote about the film in the West German *Frankfurter Allgemeine Zeitung*, it had been almost a month since its premiere. Zimmermann linked the demonstrations for democracy to the breaking of a taboo on homosexuality in *Coming Out*. To Zimmermann, the mere release of Carow's film, which succeeded in touching upon something important to the audiences at the time, was a sign of enormous social change that in some ways was just beginning.[116]

The fortieth annual Berlin International Film Festival, or Berlinale, in February 1990 was the first major international film festival to take place following the dramatic changes in East Germany. It was also the first Berlinale to be held simultaneously in both parts of the still largely divided city. The film's award and screening history illustrates its resonance both around the time of its release and continuing in recent years up to today. In 1990, *Coming Out* was selected for two awards at the Berlinale: the Silver Bear and the Teddy Award. In addition to its top prize, the Golden Bear, the Berlinale customarily awards seven Silver Bears for various categories (e.g., best screenplay, best director). *Coming Out* received the Silver Bear for Outstanding Artistic Accomplishment and was praised for the "expression of deep respect for human rights, humanity, and tolerance."[117] The Teddy Award is the leading recognition of queer filmmaking, what the Berlinale calls "a socially engaged, political honour presented to films and people who communicate queer themes on a broad social platform, thereby contributing to tolerance, acceptance, solidarity and equality in society."[118] An article about that year's Berlinale posited that the festival and its reception were strongly affected by the "impression of the political changes in the Eastern European countries."[119] *Coming Out* was specifically mentioned in many of the articles covering the festival, which noted that the film was a special attraction alongside a program of previously banned GDR films.[120] One article made light of a "herd of Silver Bears" awarded at the festival, what the author calls "prize inflation." The same article refers to the film dismissively and calls *Coming Out* an "appeal for tolerance" and its Silver Bear reluctantly "perhaps an historic win" as a film focused on a gay theme.[121] The film's appearance at the Berlinale led to its inclusion in other film festivals, including the influential New York International Festival of Lesbian and Gay Film, where it was screened in the summer of 1990 and generated a great deal of attention.[122] By June 1990, *Coming Out* had been broadcast on German television, expanding the viewership of the film even further.

As part of the film's 1989–90 release tour, Carow, Freihof, and Kummer traveled to West Germany and beyond, including the United States. The year 1990 was also the start of *Coming Out*'s long tradition of being screened at queer film festivals around the world; that year they included, in addition to New York, Los Angeles and San Francisco. The international reviews that accompanied the film's debut outside Germany, however, were not always positive. The UK *Guardian*'s review called it "ponderous."[123] Dismissing any artistic merits the film might have, the *New York Times* referred to the film as a kind of documentarian artifact, "a rare glimpse of gay life in East Germany before the crumbling of Communism."[124] Many of the other US reviews of the film were among the most unforgiving. Some of these responses to the film are unsurprising from critics unfamiliar with DEFA films, with their intense dedication to realism and slower development of narrative. A San Francisco-area reviewer wrote in a caustic piece, "Every scene goes on about four minutes too long and every take wears out its welcome—interminably."[125] Most of the negative response in the US, however, focused on the film's seeming outdatedness or its recollection of an earlier time in the development of queer liberation. Another reviewer wrote, "Not everything about *Coming Out* is as enlightened as one might like— make what you will of a tender sex scene undercut by creepy dissonant evil-dwells-here music, or by gay bar scenes rendered so grotesque they're like *Cruising* meets *The Damned*."[126] Such critical views of the film arise partly from the fact that East Germany was in a radically different position from the US with respect to representation of gay life. Yet, the US remained far from an accepting queer paradise.

Although *Coming Out* made a substantial contribution to the film history of the GDR and central and eastern Europe, the film nonetheless had other shortcomings that affected its reception and legacy. One such weakness was its treatment of women. Philipp's development as a character is the film's primary focus. This objective notwithstanding, Philipp's relationship with Tanja is shown as a contrast to the warm and accepting love he receives from Matthias. Dagmar Manzel puts in a credible performance as Tanja, but the film both sidelines the character and deploys her as part of the soul-crushing society in which Philipp cannot find acceptance of himself. Far less important to the story and customary for melodrama, there are undeveloped characters such as Philipp's mother. When Philipp visits his family home and finds his mother asleep over her typewriter in front of a poster of Bertolt Brecht, she awakens and quickly complains about the house chores that Philipp no longer completes, becoming almost a caricature of the patriarchal system whose expectations also limit Philipp's life.[127] His mother's dissatisfaction with her husband's unwillingness to help out around the home and her double burden of carrying out professional and domestic work reflect the East German official position on the state's need to support women.[128]

Another limitation of *Coming Out* is that lesbians are almost nowhere to be found in it. In 1991 Ursula Sillge, a lesbian activist who had prominently agitated for homosexual emancipation and women's rights in the GDR, wrote critically of *Coming Out*, "Naturally it was about gay men. Once more, it became apparent that everything that has to do with men gets preference."[129] While lesbians had been better represented in the documentary *The Other Love* (1988), for Sillge and others, *Coming Out*'s exclusive attention to men was another instance of lesbian erasure and discrimination against women.[130] Sillge recognizes the film's value, in that it showed a subset of society defined by and marginalized based on sexuality, but the message of the film, and its evidence of queer life in the GDR, is limited to gay men.[131] Lesbian invisibility, both in the film and in other parts of queer life, was especially frustrating since lesbians had organized and played a decisive role in one of the most effective activist programs in the early 1980s: the drive to memorialize homosexual victims of the Nazi concentration camps, which was illegal at the time.[132]

Now, more than thirty years after its premiere, *Coming Out* remains a landmark film. Thanks to the film's title and the premiere's timing, the "coming out" of Philipp and the film's subject matter have been linked, ever since 1989, to the "coming out" of East Germans into the West as the Berlin Wall fell. Indeed, one West German critic pointed out only a month after the premiere that, despite the film's heavy distribution, it had been overshadowed by the "'coming out' of an entire people."[133] This observation has recurred in the decades since then. In milestone years marking the anniversary of the fall of the Berlin Wall (1989) or German unification (1990), *Coming Out* remains a popular addition to public film screenings and is fruitful in discussions of a host of topics: East German history and society, the fall of Communist systems in the Eastern Bloc, and the history of sexuality. Around the world, the film has continued to be screened, including at events in the Republic of Georgia, Ukraine, the Czech Republic, and Russia as well as in the United States, Canada, France, and Australia.

Coming Out has a timeless yet simultaneously anachronistic quality. Some of this stems from the film's release and premiere on November 9, 1989. The outsized hopes that accompanied the film, on the part of both the filmmakers and the queer viewers who looked forward to some kind of representation, were doomed to be overshadowed by the more newsworthy events of that day and the weeks that followed. Although *Coming Out* did receive a fair amount of attention, its message became tangled in the meaning of the collapse of the GDR and what many saw as the colonization of East Germany by a triumphalist capitalist West Germany. Practically, this meant that any reforms or reform-oriented discussions the filmmakers wanted to inspire either could not take place or had to take a different legal, political, and social form, because they occurred in the radically different context of the new Germany. For LGBTQ+ viewers in various national and cultural environments, *Coming Out* remains meaningful for both its record of prejudices and its reminder that such discrimination remains, even if in different form, more than thirty years later. The film's other messages about belonging and social exclusion are significant for all viewers, communicating what Heiner Carow often wanted his films to convey: that societies are complex structures and require individual and collective action to ensure that no one is left behind or pushed out.

CREDITS

Director:
Heiner Carow

Assistant Directors:
Hanna Seydel
Dirk Kummer

Writer:
Wolfram Witt

Production Company:
DEFA Studio for Feature Films

Production Leader:
Horst Hartwig

Cast:
Matthias Freihof (Philipp)
Dagmar Manzel (Tanja)
Dirk Kummer (Matthias)
Michael Gwisdek (Achim)
Werner Dissel (Walter)
Gudrun Ritter (Frau Möllemann and
    waitress)
Walfriede Schmitt (Philipp's mother)
Axel Wandtke (Jakob)
Pierre Sanoussi-Bliss (Black man)
René Schmidt (Young man from the park)
Robert Hummel (Lutz)

Music:
Stefan Carow

Cinematography:
Martin Schlesinger

Film Editing:
Evelyn Carow

Production Design:
Georg Wratsch

Costume Design:
Regina Viertel

Runtime:
113 min.

Sound Mix:
Mono

Color:
ORWO and Kodak Color

Aspect Ratio:
1.66 : 1

Film Length:
3,078 m

Negative Format:
35 mm

Cinematographic Process:
Spherical

Printed Film Format:
35 mm

Production Costs:
M 2,615,000

Release Dates:
November 1989 (German Democratic
    Republic), February 1990 (Federal
    Republic of Germany), February 1991
    (USA)

NOTES

1   I frequently use "LGBTQ+" (lesbian, gay, bisexual, trans, and beyond) and "queer" as descriptors in this text for two main reasons. First, they are more inclusive labels for various identities both in and not represented in the film. Second, although the film focuses on putative gay men's experiences, a wider range of individuals appears in the film, and it was the goal of the filmmakers to address more than only gay men. As I write later, however, this was still to the detriment of women's, specifically lesbians', experiences. Further, there were multiple classifications in circulation in the GDR, including the equivalents of "homophile" and "homosexually inclined."

2   Ute Wölfel, "Not Just Death and Ruins: The Young, and New Beginnings in German 'Rubble Films,'" *German Life and Letters* 69, no. 4 (2016): 503–18.

3   Sebastian Heiduschke, *East German Cinema: DEFA and Film History* (New York: Palgrave Macmillan, 2013), 143n25.

4   Andrea Rinke, "From Models to Misfits: Women in DEFA Films of the 1970s and 1980s," in *DEFA: East German Cinema, 1946–1992*, ed. Seán Allan and John Sandford (New York: Berghahn Books, 1999), 191.

5   Rosemary Stott, "'Letting the Genie Out of the Bottle': DEFA Film-Makers and *Film und Fernsehen*," in *DEFA: East German Cinema, 1946–1992*, ed. Allan and Sandford (New York: Berghahn Books, 1999), 47–52.

6   Heiner Carow, "Es ist Zeit, über das Kino nachzudenken," *Film und Fernsehen* 4, no. 2 (1976): 15.

7   Heiner Carow, interview by Axel Geiss, September 1994, 1, Schwules Museum Archive, Berlin, DDR/Coming Out, Nr. 4.

8   Erika Richter, "Nachruf für Heiner Carow," *Film und Fernsehen* 25, no. 1 (1997): 3.

9   For more on *The Other Love*, see Kyle Frackman, "Shame and Love: East German Homosexuality Goes to the Movies," in *Gender and Sexuality in East German Film: Intimacy and Alienation*, ed. Kyle Frackman and Faye Stewart (Rochester, NY: Camden House, 2018), 225–48.

10 Peter Claus, "Toleranz, die täglich neu zu üben ist: JW-Gespräch zum neuen DEFA-Film 'Coming out,'" *Junge Welt*, November 4, 1989.

11 Heiduschke, *East German Cinema*, 15.

12 Erich Honecker, "Zu aktuellen Fragen bei der Verwirklichung der Beschlüsse unseres VIII. Parteitages," *Neues Deutschland*, December 18, 1971, ZEFYS Zeitungsportal.

13 Kurt Starke, "Gutachten zum Treatment 'Coming out' Witt/Richter 3.12.87," April 5, 1988, 2, Bundesarchiv (BArch, Federal Archive) DR 117/7747.

14 Starke, "Gutachten zum Treatment," 4.

15 Maria Planitzer, "Gutachten zu 'Coming out,'" April 21, 1988, 1, BArch DR 117/7747.

16 Karl-Heinz Schöneburg, "Gutachten zu dem Film-Szenarium 'Coming out,'" April 27, 1988, 1–2, BArch DR 117/7747.

17 Planitzer, "Gutachten," 2; Schöneburg, "Gutachten," 4–5.

18 Heiner Carow, "Regiekonzeption für *Coming Out*," December 13, 1988, BArch DR 117/12391; Horst Hartwig, "'Coming out' Production Documents (4/5)," October 28, 1988, BArch DR 117/29722.

19 19 Michel Foucault, *The Birth of Biopolitics: Lectures at the Collège de France, 1978–79*, ed. Michel Senellart, trans. Graham Burchell (Houndmills, UK: Palgrave Macmillan, 2008), 21–22; Jasbir K. Puar, *The Right to Maim: Debility, Capacity, Disability* (Durham, NC: Duke University Press, 2017), xviii.

20 Stephen Best, *None Like Us: Blackness, Belonging, Aesthetic Life* (Durham, NC: Duke University Press, 2018), 7.

21 Udo Grashoff, "Driven into Suicide by the East German Regime? Reflections on the Persistence of a Misleading Perception," *Central European History* 52, no. 2 (2019): 311.

22 The higher prevalence of suicide in the GDR may be linked to longstanding regional behaviors among the population that predate the GDR. See Grashoff, "Driven into Suicide," 331.

23 Christopher Ingraham, *Gestures of Concern* (Durham, NC: Duke University Press, 2020), 2.

24 Denis M. Sweet, "Bodies for Germany, Bodies for Socialism: The German Democratic Republic Devises a Gay (Male) Body," in *Gender and Germanness: Cultural Productions of a Nation*, ed. Patricia Herminghouse and Magda Mueller (Providence, RI: Berghahn Books, 1997), 253.

25 David Brandon Dennis, "*Coming Out* into Socialism: Heiner Carow's Third Way," in *A Companion to German Cinema*, ed. Terri Ginsberg and Andrea Mensch (Malden, MA: Blackwell, 2012), 73.

26 Eve Kosofsky Sedgwick, *Epistemology of the Closet* (Berkeley: University of California Press, 1990), 3.

27 John Mercer and Martin Shingler, *Melodrama: Genre, Style, Sensibility* (New York: Wallflower, 2004), 2.

28 Thomas Elsaesser, "Tales of Sound and Fury: Observations on the Family Melodrama," in *Imitations of Life: A Reader on Film & Television Melodrama*, ed. Marcia Landy (Detroit: Wayne State University Press, 1991), 69.

29 Anke Pinkert, "Can Melodrama Cure? War Trauma and Crisis of Masculinity in Early DEFA Film," *Seminar: A Journal of Germanic Studies* 44, no. 1 (2008): 118–19.

30 Barton Byg, "DEFA and the Traditions of International Cinema," in *DEFA: East German Cinema, 1946–1992*, ed. Allan and Sandford (New York: Berghahn Books, 1999), 30.

31   Laura Heins, *Nazi Film Melodrama* (Urbana: University of Illinois Press, 2013), 3.

32   Hester Baer, *German Cinema in the Age of Neoliberalism* (Amsterdam: Amsterdam University Press, 2021), 216, https://www.jstor.org/stable/10.2307/j.ctv1hp5hnv.

33   Jonathan Goldberg, *Melodrama: An Aesthetics of Impossibility* (Durham, NC: Duke University Press, 2016), 33.

34   Goldberg, *Melodrama*, 4.

35   Goldberg, *Melodrama*, 39.

36   Goldberg, *Melodrama*, 4.

37   Goldberg, *Melodrama*, 9.

38   Goldberg, *Melodrama*, x.

39   Katrin Sieg, "Homosexualität und Dissidenz: Zur Freiheit der Liebe in Heiner Carows *Coming Out*," in *Die imaginierte Nation: Identität, Körper und Geschlecht in DEFA-Filmen*, ed. Bettina Mathes (Berlin: DEFA-Stiftung, 2007), 284.

40   Goldberg, *Melodrama*, 8; Peter Brooks, *The Melodramatic Imagination: Balzac, Henry James, Melodrama, and the Mode of Excess* (New Haven, CT: Yale University Press, 1976), xi, 4.

41   Wolfram Witt, "'Coming out': Drehbuch," September 19, 1988, 13, BArch DR 117/2418.

42   Tom Gunning, "Mechanisms of Laughter: The Devices of Slapstick," in *Slapstick Comedy*, ed. Tom Paulus and Rob King (New York: Routledge, 2010), 138.

43   Gunning, "Mechanisms of Laughter," 139; Louise Peacock, *Slapstick and Comic Performance: Comedy and Pain* (New York: Palgrave Macmillan, 2014), 31–32; Ervin Malakaj and Alena E. Lyons, "Introduction: Interdisciplinary Approaches to Slapstick," in *Slapstick: An Interdisciplinary Companion*, ed. Ervin Malakaj and Alena E. Lyons (Berlin: De Gruyter, 2021), 1–3.

44   Tamar Jeffers McDonald, *Romantic Comedy: Boy Meets Girl Meets Genre* (London: Wallflower, 2007), 9.

45   McDonald, *Romantic Comedy*, 11, 118.

46   McDonald, *Romantic Comedy*, 12.

47   David R. Shumway, *Modern Love: Romance, Intimacy, and the Marriage Crisis* (New York: New York University Press, 2003), 26.

48   Kyle Stevens, "Romantic Comedy and the Virtues of Predictability," *New Review of Film and Television Studies* 18, no. 1 (2020): 28–48.

49   Stevens, "Romantic Comedy," 45–46.

50   McDonald, *Romantic Comedy*, 59, 62.

51   Jack Halberstam, *Female Masculinity*, 2nd ed. (Durham, NC: Duke University Press, 2018), 100.

52 Philip Thomson, "'Exegi Momentum': The Fame of Bertolt Brecht," *German Quarterly* 53, no. 3 (1980): 337–38.

53 Bertolt Brecht, "Ich benötige keinen Grabstein," in *Bertolt Brecht: Die Gedichte*, ed. Jan Knopf (Frankfurt am Main: Insel Verlag, 2008), 973.

54 Sedgwick, *Epistemology*, 70.

55 Witt, "'Coming out': Drehbuch," 42.

56 Peter Ulrich Weiß, "Civil Society from the Underground: The Alternative Antifa Network in the GDR," *Journal of Urban History* 41, no. 4 (2015): 649.

57 Britta Bugiel, *Rechtsextremismus Jugendlicher in der DDR und in den neuen Bundesländern von 1982–1998* (Münster: Lit Verlag, 2002), 81.

58 Audre Lorde, *The Collected Poems of Audre Lorde* (New York: W. W. Norton, 1997), 465; Audre Lorde, *The Marvelous Arithmetics of Distance: Poems 1987–1992* (New York: W. W. Norton, 1993).

59 Baer, *German Cinema*, 223.

60 The later script version discussed below resembles the earlier draft: Wolfram Witt, "'Coming out': Szenarium," ed. Erika Richter, April 14, 1988, BArch DR 117/7060.

61 Witt, "'Coming out': Drehbuch," 1–4.

62 Witt, "'Coming out': Drehbuch," 5.

63 Witt, "'Coming out': Drehbuch," 8.

64 Witt, "'Coming out': Drehbuch," 11.

65 Not long after appearing in *Coming Out*, Mahlsdorf starred in Rosa von Praunheim's 1992 film *I Am My Own Woman* (*Ich bin meine eigene Frau*), an adaptation of Mahlsdorf's autobiography of the same title (also published in 1992). That film includes a clip from *Coming Out*, and, like the rest of the film, Mahlsdorf recalls the events and reenacts dramatized versions of them. Heiner Carow and Dirk Kummer appear in one scene with her and add to Mahlsdorf's recollections of the simultaneous premiere and opening of the GDR's borders.

66 Ilona Rühmann, "Rauskommen," *Neue Berliner Illustrierte*, November 1989, 26.

67 Henryk Goldberg, "Coming Out," *Filmspiegel* (February 1989): 4.

68 "Coming out—Pressematerial" (DEFA-Aussenhandel, 1989), 6, Schwules Museum Archive, Berlin, DDR, Nr. 3.

69 Karsten Troyke is an actor, voice actor, and musician known especially for his recordings of Yiddish songs.

70 Kathryn Hellerstein, "Introduction," in *Paper Bridges: Selected Poems of Kadya Molodowsky*, trans. Hellerstein (Detroit: Wayne State University Press, 1999), 18. Copyright © 1999 Wayne State University Press, used with the permission of Wayne State University Press.

71   Kadya Molodowsky, *Paper Bridges: Selected Poems of Kadya Molodowsky*, trans. Kathryn Hellerstein (Detroit: Wayne State University Press, 1999), 327–28. Copyright © 1999 Wayne State University Press, used with the permission of Wayne State University Press.

72   Thomas C. Fox, *Stated Memory: East Germany and the Holocaust* (Rochester, NY: Camden House, 1999), 9.

73   Cora Granata, "The Cold War Politics of Cultural Minorities: Jews and Sorbs in the German Democratic Republic, 1976–1989," *German History* 27, no. 1 (2009): 60–61.

74   Birgit Wolf, *Sprache in der DDR: Ein Wörterbuch* (Berlin: De Gruyter, 2013), 247.

75   Richard Dyer, *Nino Rota: Music, Film and Feeling* (Basingstoke, UK: Palgrave Macmillan/British Film Institute, 2010), 10.

76   Jean-Paul Sartre, *Critique of Dialectical Reason*, ed. Jonathan Rée, trans. Alan Sheridan-Smith, vol. 1 (London: Verso, 2004), 256.

77   Joe Moran, *Reading the Everyday* (London: Routledge, 2005), 1.

78   Katherine Verdery, *What Was Socialism, and What Comes Next?* (Princeton, NJ: Princeton University Press, 1996), 46.

79   Verdery, *What Was Socialism*, 46, 57.

80   Anna Fishzon, "Queue Time as Queer Time: An Occasion for Pleasure and Desire in the Brezhnev Era and Today," *Slavic & East European Journal* 61, no. 3 (2017): 544; Jack Halberstam, *In a Queer Time and Place: Transgender Bodies, Subcultural Lives* (New York: New York University Press, 2005).

81   Donna Harsch, *Revenge of the Domestic: Women, the Family, and Communism in the German Democratic Republic* (Princeton, NJ: Princeton University Press, 2007), 199; Josie McLellan, "From Private Photography to Mass Circulation: The Queering of East German Visual Culture, 1968–1989," *Central European History* 48, no. 3 (2015): 407.

82   Josie McLellan, "'Even under Socialism, We Don't Want to Do without Love': East German Erotica," in *Pleasures in Socialism: Leisure and Luxury in the Eastern Bloc*, ed. David Crowley and Susan E. Reid (Evanston, IL: Northwestern University Press, 2010), 223.

83   Josie McLellan, *Love in the Time of Communism: Intimacy and Sexuality in the GDR* (Cambridge: Cambridge University Press, 2011), 139.

84   Witt, "'Coming out': Drehbuch," 137–38.

85   Dennis, "*Coming Out* into Socialism," 71.

86   Witt, "'Coming out': Drehbuch," 149.

87   Heinz Bulmahn, "Ideology, Family Policy, Production, and (Re)Education: Literary Treatment of Abortion in the GDR of the Early 1980s," *Studies in 20th & 21st Century Literature* 21, no. 2 (1997): 317–18.

88 Pamela Fisher, "Abortion in Post-Communist Germany: The End of Muttipolitik and a Still Birth [*sic*] for Feminism," *Women's Studies International Forum* 28, no. 1 (2005): 21–36.

89 Samuel K. N. Blay and Ryszard W. Piotrowicz, "The Advance of German Unification and the Abortion Debate," *Statute Law Review* 14, no. 3 (1993): 177.

90 The *Christmas Oratorio* was performed in the film by the Singakademie Berlin choir and the Weimar Staatskapelle orchestra under the direction of Dietrich Knothe.

91 Markus Rathey, *Johann Sebastian Bach's* Christmas Oratorio*: Music, Theology, Culture* (New York: Oxford University Press, 2016), 10, 48.

92 Witt, "'Coming out': Drehbuch," 192.

93 Witt, "'Coming out': Drehbuch," 193.

94 Sarah Ensor, "Queer Fallout: Samuel R. Delany and the Ecology of Cruising," *Environmental Humanities* 9, no. 1 (2017): 155.

95 Alice A. Kuzniar, "Zarah Leander and Transgender Specularity," *Film Criticism* 23, no. 2/3 (1999): 74–93.

96 Alan Lareau, "Lavender Songs: Undermining Gender in Weimar Cabaret and Beyond," *Popular Music and Society* 28, no. 1 (2005): 27.

97 Dennis, "*Coming Out* into Socialism," 74.

98 Heiner Carow et al., *Heiner Carow "Coming Out" (DDR, 1988/89): Filmgespräch*, Cassette, 1989, Akademie der Künste, Berlin, Medienarchiv, AVM-31 2751.

99 Starke, "Gutachten zum Treatment," 4.

100 Witt, "'Coming out': Drehbuch," 207–8.

101 Goldberg, *Melodrama*, 4.

102 Ingrid Poss and Peter Warnecke, eds., *Spur der Filme: Zeitzeugen über die DEFA* (Berlin: Ch. Links Verlag, 2006), 453.

103 Hans Dieter Mäde, "Stellungnahme zum Film 'Coming out,'" July 5, 1989, 3, BArch DR 117/29796.

104 Helmut Diller, "Stellungnahme zur Staatlichen Zulassung des Films 'Coming out,'" July 25, 1989, 1, BArch DR 117/29796.

105 Winfried Schade, "Stellungnahme des Verleihs zur Staatlichen Zulassung des Films 'Coming out' aus dem DEFA-Studio für Spielfilme," July 25, 1989, 1–2, BArch DR 117/29796.

106 For example, Progress Film-Verleih, "Neu im Kino," *Neues Deutschland*, November 2, 1989, 7, ZEFYS Zeitungsportal.

107 Steven Geyer, "'Coming Out': Die Party der Anderen," *Frankfurter Rundschau*, November 6, 2014, sec. Politik, http://www.fr-online.de/politik/-coming-out--die-party-der-anderen,1472596,28967274.html.

108 Carow et al., *Heiner Carow "Coming Out" (DDR, 1988/89): Filmgespräch.*

109 Vito Russo, "From Screen to Shining Screen: The Richness of Gay Life Is Celebrated at Film Festivals," *Advocate*, July 3, 1990, 68.

110 Norbert Jesse, "Ehrlichkeit in Beziehungen ist nicht spielbar," *Neue Zeit*, November 9, 1989, sec. Aus dem kulturellen Leben, 4, ZEFYS Zeitungsportal.

111 "DDR-Regierung erklärte ihren Rücktritt," *Berliner Zeitung*, November 8, 1989, 1, ZEFYS Zeitungsportal.

112 Günter Sobe, "Ein Film als Toleranz-Edikt: DEFA-Uraufführung—Carows 'Coming out,'" *Berliner Zeitung*, November 10, 1989, sec. Kulturpolitik, 7, ZEFYS Zeitungsportal.

113 Helmut Ullrich, "Von Menschen, die anders als andere sind: 'Coming out'—Film von Heiner Carow," *Neue Zeit*, November 10, 1989, 4, ZEFYS Zeitungsportal.

114 Horst Knietzsch, "Nachdenken über Widerstreit der Gefühle: Premiere von Heiner Carows neuem Film 'Coming out' in Berlin," *Neues Deutschland*, November 11, 1989, sec. Politik/Kultur, 12, ZEFYS Zeitungsportal.

115 Peter Claus, "Die läuternde Kraft tosender Gefühle: Heiner Carows neuer DEFA-Film 'Coming out' hatte Premiere mit viel Beifall, Lob und—wie normal—Widerspruch," *Junge Welt*, November 11, 1989, 5, Schwules Museum Archive, Berlin, DDR/Coming Out, Nr. 4.

116 Monika Zimmermann, "Wo Schranken fallen: DDR-Film bricht ein Tabu," *Frankfurter Allgemeine Zeitung*, December 1, 1989, 33.

117 "Preise & Auszeichnungen 1990," *Internationale Filmfestspiele Berlin*, accessed August 6, 2020, https://www.berlinale.de/de/archiv/jahresarchive/1990/03_preistraeger_1990/03_preistraeger_1990.html; "Filmdetails: *Coming out*," *DEFA-Stiftung*, 2018, https://www.defa-stiftung.de/filme/filmsuche/coming-out/.

118 "Prizes of the Independent Juries," *Berlin International Film Festival*, accessed January 24, 2020, https://www.berlinale.de/en/festival/awards-and-juries/independent-juries.html.

119 Klaus M. Fiedler, "Gespannte Erwartung auf schillerndes Film-Fest: Vorschau auf die heute beginnende 40. Berlinale," *Neue Zeit*, February 9, 1990, sec. Aus dem kulturellen Leben, 4, ZEFYS Zeitungsportal.

120 Horst Knietzsch, "Die Berlinale ist eröffnet: Festspiele erstmalig in beiden Teilen der Stadt," *Neues Deutschland*, February 10, 1990, sec. Kultur, 5, ZEFYS Zeitungsportal. The previously banned or censored films shown at the 1990 Berlinale included *Born in '45* (*Jahrgang '45*, 1949, dir. Jürgen Böttcher), *Don't Think I'll Cry* (*Denk bloß nicht, ich heule*, 1965, dir. Frank Vogel), *When You Are Grown Up, Dear Adam* (*Wenn du groß bist, Lieber Adam*, 1965, dir. Egon Günter), *The Rabbit Is Me* (*Das Kaninchen bin ich*, 1965, dir. Kurt Maetzig), *Berlin around the Corner* (*Berlin um die Ecke*, 1966, dir. Gerhard Klein), and *Trace of Stones* (*Spur der Steine*, 1966, dir. Frank Beyer).

121 Günter Sobe, "Berlinale—Nach der Großen Pause: Ende der 40. Internationalen Film-festspiele Berlin," *Berliner Zeitung*, February 22, 1990, sec. Kultur, 7, ZEFYS Zeitungs-portal.

122 Stephen Holden, "Gay and Lesbian Festival Widens Its Film Horizons," *New York Times*, May 31, 1990, C18.

123 Derek Malcolm, "Invasion of the Movie Snatchers: Will Hollywood Kill Eastern Euro-pean Cinema?," *Guardian*, February 15, 1990.

124 Holden, "Gay and Lesbian Festival," C18.

125 Warren Sonbert, "Gay in Germany before Wall Fell," *Bay Area Reporter*, June 14, 1990.

126 "Gay Fest: Bravery, Anger, and Poetry," *SF Weekly*, June 13, 1990, 1, 11, 18.

127 Baer, *German Cinema*, 222.

128 Susanne Kranz, "Women's Role in the German Democratic Republic and the State's Policy toward Women," *Journal of International Women's Studies* 7, no. 1 (2005): 69–83.

129 Ursula Sillge, *Un-Sichtbare Frauen: Lesben und ihre Emanzipation in der DDR* (Berlin: LinksDruck Verlag, 1991), 16.

130 For more on lesbian representation in the GDR and efforts to document it, see Maria Bühner, "How to Remember Invisibility: Documentary Projects on Lesbians in the German Democratic Republic as Archives of Feelings," in *Sexual Culture in Germany in the 1970s: A Golden Age for Queers?*, ed. Janin Afken and Benedikt Wolf (Cham, Switzerland: Palgrave Macmillan, 2019), 241–65.

131 Sillge, *Un-Sichtbare Frauen*, 20.

132 See Erik N. Jensen, "The Pink Triangle and Political Consciousness: Gays, Lesbians, and the Memory of Nazi Persecution," *Journal of the History of Sexuality* 11, no. 1 (Janu-ary 1, 2002): 336n85.

133 Heinz Kersten, "Ein Modellfall für anderes: Heiner Carows neuer DEFA-Film 'Com-ing out,'" *Der Tagesspiegel*, November 26, 1989.